NOW WHAT?

YOUR
NEXT
STEPS
AFTER
SAYING
YES
TO
JESUS

MATT MCCARTY

Now What? – Your Next Steps After Saying Yes to Jesus
Copyright © 2022 by Matt Mccarty

ISBN: 978-0-9863242-7-7

Published by McCarty Ministries
P.O. Box 602
Portage, MI 49081
www.mccartyministries.com

Cover design by Bethany Kruzan

ENDORSEMENTS

"I have known Matt McCarty for almost 20 years, and he is the real deal. Matt is a gifted writer and Bible teacher with a passion to help young people experience a genuine relationship with the Lord. Through his newest book, *Now What?* — loaded with humor, practical tips, engaging stories and the Word — Matt helps students discover the necessary steps to developing a vibrant relationship with God. This is a must-have book for every young person (and parents, too) and I highly recommend it!"

— Beth Jones, Author of *Getting a Grip on the Basics* and Co-Founding Senior Pastor, Valley Family Church

"I loved reading Matt McCarty's book, *Now What – Your Next Steps After Saying Yes to Jesus.* I was not only impressed with the excellent content he shared, but I thoroughly enjoyed his fresh and relevant communication style. It made me wish someone had given me this book decades ago when I first encountered Jesus in my teen years. It would have helped me tremendously to have such practical guidelines for spiritual growth. People, young and old, need to know that accepting Jesus is not some "final step," but rather, it's a first step in a lifelong walk with God. Matt's book will really help people with that."

— Tony Cooke, Bible Teacher, Tony Cooke Ministries and Author of *In Search of Timothy* and *Lift: Experiencing the Elevated Life*

PRAYER OF SALVATION

This book is designed as a guide to new Christians on what steps they need to take to keep their newfound faith going. If you haven't already said a prayer of salvation to make Jesus the Lord of your life, I'd encourage you to do that right now. Doing so is both the FIRST and MOST IMPORTANT step you can take.

Below is a very simple prayer you can pray to get started. Once you have finished praying this prayer, please share what you did with someone you love and trust. They'll be able to celebrate with you and show you what to do next. Read the following out loud as a prayer to God:

Father God,

I come to you today and recognize that I am a sinner in need of a savior. I believe the truth of the Bible that says that all people have fallen short of your glory. I believe that without Jesus, I would go to Hell when I die. I also believe the truth of the bible that says a person must first believe in Jesus, and then confess Him as Lord to be saved. I want to do that, right now.

Father, forgive me of all my sins. I'm sorry for trying to live life by my own rules. Today I choose to live by yours from now on. Jesus, I need you. I confess you as both Lord and savior of my life. Change me. Help me. Heal me. Love me. Guide me.

I love you, Lord. Thank you for hearing and answering my prayer! I'm grateful to you for what you have done for me, and for the chance to spend the rest of my life with you on Earth and in Heaven.

In Jesus' name, amen!

Congratulations! Welcome to the family of God! Now, let's find out what to do next by diving into Now What? – Your Next Steps After Saying *Yes* to Jesus.

CONTENTS

INTRODUCTION

Congratulations! You just made the most important decision you'll ever make in your life. You made the decision to accept Jesus as your personal Lord and Savior. This decision is more important than choosing the right college or job after high school. It's more important than choosing the person you'll marry. It's more important than picking the right outfit for school every morning. And it's more important than choosing what to do on Friday night. By accepting Jesus as your personal Lord and Savior, you have joined over two billion other people on earth. That's right—two billion people! You're now part of a global family of people who are called Christians, Christ followers, or Jesus followers.

At this point, you're probably wondering what to do next. This book is designed to show you the practical steps you can and should take to make sure your life as a Christian is rewarding and successful. You probably have a ton of questions about the decision you made. You're also probably experiencing a bunch of emotions. We'll help walk you through all your questions and show you how to work through those emotions. The truth is, becoming a Christian is the easy part. Living out this life every single day is a little more challenging, but you can do it! Two billion other people are doing the same thing. More importantly, Jesus is now living with you and helping you along this journey. Plus, your friends and family at church and in your youth group can help as well.

AT THIS POINT, YOU'RE PROBABLY WONDERING WHAT TO DO NEXT.

WHAT JUST HAPPENED?

Let's answer the first question you're asking: What just happened? Christians say that what you just experienced is the act of being born again. But what does that really mean? The Bible is where Christians get the term *born again*; it comes from the words of Jesus. Jesus says, "So don't be surprised when I say, 'You must be born again.'"[1]

Jesus is teaching Nicodemus that in order to enter Heaven upon death, he must become "born again." Those of us alive today live *after* the death, burial, and resurrection of Jesus, the act of substitution that made the way for us. This means we can also act on what Jesus tells Nicodemus to do. By saying the prayer you said, and by believing in your heart what you heard about Jesus, you became born again and decided to live your life for Him. You decided to read the Bible, live the way it teaches, and let Jesus take the reins of control in your life. With your prayer, you made Jesus the Lord and Savior of your life. He is Lord because He now leads your life. And He is Savior because He saved you from the penalties of sin. Those penalties include, pain, fear, sickness, death, and living forever in hell. You're now born again, your destination after death is Heaven, and it is a miracle!

Jesus is teaching Nicodemus what must be done and says to become "born again." Those of us alive today live *after* the death, burial, and resurrection of Jesus. This means we can act on what Jesus tells Nicodemus to do. By saying the prayer you said, and by believing in your heart what you heard about Jesus, you decided to live your life like Him. You decided to read the Bible, live the way it teaches, and let Jesus take the reins of control in your life. With your prayer, you made Jesus the Lord and Savior of your life. He is Lord because He now leads your life. And He is Savior because He saved you from the penalties of sin. Those penalties include living forever in hell. You're now born again, and it is a miracle!

But how can you be born again? After all, your mom didn't give birth to you a second time (which would be *so* weird), and there were no doctors around when you said your prayer. Obviously, nothing really happened to you *physically*, but a ton of stuff did happen to you *spiritually*. Specifically speaking, something happened to your spirit, and soon things will start happening to your soul. Let's start off by talking about how you're a three-part person.

THREE-PART PERSON

While there is only one you, that *you* is a three-part person.

Did you know that? This concept is a little hard to understand because you're most familiar with the PHYSICAL part of you. It's your physical body that everyone sees and talks to. It's your physical body that gets tired. It's your physical body that gets hungry. It's your physical body you see in the mirror. So how can you have three parts? One part is easily seen, yet the other two parts are somewhat invisible.

We get the idea of your three-part nature from the Bible. It says, "Now may the God of peace make you holy in every way and may your whole SPIRIT and SOUL and BODY be kept blameless until our Lord Jesus Christ comes again"[2] (emphasis added). Notice how this Bible verse lists three different parts of a person. Paul's prayer is that the church members' spirits, souls, and bodies are made holy in God's peace. While Paul is talking about church members he was writing to at the time, we can assume that you also have a spirit, soul and body.

THE CHICKEN EGG

A great analogy to understand your three-part nature is to consider a chicken egg. You're like a chicken egg. I know this sounds weird, but stay with me for a minute. If you were to crack open an egg, you'd see that it has three parts. First, you have the outside part of the egg known as the shell. It's the part of the egg you can see and touch. Next, you have the part of the egg that the yolk sits in. This part of the egg is known as the egg white. You don't see the egg white unless you crack open the egg. Next, you have the yolk inside of the egg white. Again, it's not something you see unless you dissect the three layers.

Each part of the egg exists on its own and in partnership with the other two parts. All three parts together make up the whole egg. The shell is what allows the egg to exist. Without the shell, the egg white and yoke would just spill all over the place. The egg white is what gives the egg its character. It's what surrounds the yoke and can be eaten in several forms. It can be scrambled or hard boiled. The yoke is the part of the egg that has life inside of it. The yoke is the core of the egg. It eventually changes to a baby chick if it is fertilized.

BODY

You're a SPIRIT, you have a SOUL, and you live in a physical BODY. Your physical body is like the egg's shell. Your body is what others can see. It allows you to live on this planet and gives your soul and your spirit a "house" to live in. While your body is what others talk to, play games with, and hang out with; it isn't the real you. Think of it this way—when someone dies, their body goes into the ground, but the real person still lives on. Inside your physical body is a soul and a spirit.

SOUL

Your soul is made up of your mind, will, and emotions. Your soul is what gives you your character or personality. Your mind is where all your thinking, believing, and processing happens—much like how a computer works. When you're in math class and you're trying to solve a problem in your head, it happens in your mind. When you're in math class and you're daydreaming about something instead of trying to solve the problem, it happens in your mind. While your mind's processing happens within your brain, your mind is something that a person cannot see. In other words, no one can see what you're thinking about . . . and sometimes that's a good thing!

Your will is also part of your soul. Your will is also something that nobody can see. People can see the actions of your will but not your will itself. For example, you might not want to get out of bed in the morning to get ready for school. While your parents can see that

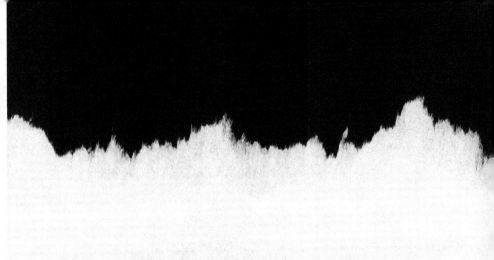

"GOD will never MAKE you
do anything because
He made your will FREE."

you're sleeping in, they can't see what is processing within the will part of your soul. They can't see your internal desire to stay warm under the covers. They can't view the theater of your soul that is imagining all the things you have to do at school today but don't want to do. Your will is the one thing that God can't and won't override.

God will never *make* you do anything because He made your will free. Your will is what decides to do right or wrong. Your will is what decides to give in to temptation or to overcome it. Your will is what decides to tell the truth or lie. It is your will that decided to make Jesus your personal Lord and Savior.

The final part of your soul is your emotions. One of the coolest traits that God gave humans was their ability to show emotions. Your emotions include things like love, anger, and sadness. Think of the Disney film *Inside Out*. Emotions are what make you cry at a sad movie or get angry when someone hurts your feelings.

Emotions make life interesting and complicated. You probably don't like when you get angry, or you might be embarrassed when you're sad. Emotions cannot be trusted because they always change. Our emotions are influenced by circumstances and therefore can change quickly and often. When you make the basketball team, you're happy. When you fail your history test, you're sad. When you scratch your parents' car, you're scared. Notice how quickly your emotions can change.

EMOTIONS MAKE LIFE INTERESTING AND COMPLICATED.

SPIRIT

As I said before, the real you (your spirit) lives in a physical body. Your body is the physical part of you that people can see and relate with. Your body helps you live on this planet. It's kind of like an "earth suit." You have a soul which includes your mind, will, and emotions. Your soul gives you your personality and is also known as your heart or deepest being. Your soul is where Jesus takes up residence. Finally, you're a spirit. Notice, I didn't say you *have* a spirit. You are a spirit because your spirit is the real you. Your spirit is what lives on in eternity either in heaven or in hell.

I can't explain *where* your spirit is within your body or *what* it exactly looks like. The Bible isn't completely clear on that. We do know that the Bible often uses the word *heart* to convey the idea of your spirit. And we know that when your spirit is talking to you, it happens in your heart (or the deepest part of your being). For example, when you do something you know you shouldn't and then you get that uneasy feeling down in your stomach area, that is your spirit talking to you. So maybe your spirit is somewhere in your gut or stomach. It doesn't really matter. What matters is that you know that you're three parts, and the real you is your spirit.

We also know that your spirit is the real you; it's the part of you that is eternal or never ends. Your spirit is what lives forever. When our bodies die, our spirit lives on in either heaven or hell. Have you ever known someone who died? Did you go to their funeral? Did they have an open casket? Do you remember how they looked kind of like the person but something was different? The reason they looked different is because the real person left their body. The life of the person was no longer in their physical body.

The Bible has a lot to say about the human spirit. I won't cover all of it, but I wanted to point out a couple of things to help you better understand this part of you. The Bible calls your spirit "the hidden person of the heart."[3] This is where we get the idea of inviting Jesus to live in your heart, not the physical heart that pumps blood but the deepest part of you.

Proverbs teaches us to "guard your heart above all else"[4] because it's where all the issues of life come from. When you made Jesus your personal Lord and Savior, He moved into your heart. That's what the process of becoming born again does; it gives Jesus permission to make a home in your heart or spirit. He could talk to you before you were born again, but He didn't have permission to live *in* you yet.

Giving Jesus permission to live in your heart, also known as saying the prayer of salvation, takes your spirit and gives it new life. Your spirit becomes born again by being reunited with God. It used to be separated from God, but now it's reconnected. It used to be destined for hell, but now it's destined for heaven.

BUT, WHAT JUST HAPPENED?

So, back to your original question—what exactly happened when you prayed the prayer to make Jesus your personal Lord and Savior? As we mentioned before, nothing really changed PHYSICALLY but a few things changed SPIRITUALLY. And soon, through Jesus' influence, things will start to change in your SOUL (mind / will / emotions). The most important thing that changed is your destination after leaving earth. Your destination changed from hell to heaven. We also said that Jesus entered your heart/spirit and made a home. That means He now lives inside your heart. Since Jesus lives inside your heart, it's now easier for Him to talk to you!

INFLUENCING YOUR MIND

Not only can Jesus talk to your heart, but He can also influence your soul in a few ways. Remember, your soul is your mind, will, and emotions. Both Jesus and your new heart can help you think the right things with your mind. Now, you don't have to think thoughts that you shouldn't think. For example, you don't have to think about cheating on your science test. Instead, Jesus can help you think about ways to study that will help you pass the test. You don't have to think about viewing websites on the Internet that you shouldn't. Instead, Jesus can help you overcome those tempting thoughts by reminding you of how dangerous and destructive they are.

INFLUENCING YOUR WILL

Because Jesus lives inside your heart, He can help you exercise your free will in a way that is healthy and godly. Instead of ignoring your parents' wish for you to clean your room because you don't feel like it, Jesus can encourage you by putting desires in your heart to honor your parents. Remember, He won't *make* you do anything, but He will speak to you and encourage you. While your will may want to binge watch your favorite show on Netflix, Jesus will motivate you in your heart to spend time in prayer and Bible reading instead.

INFLUENCING YOUR EMOTIONS

Since Jesus lives inside your heart, He can also help you understand and manage your emotions in a healthy way. For example, He can teach you through the Bible how to respond to frustrating events in a way that doesn't end in anger. He can encourage you and give you peace when you face things that would normally make you sad. When you said that prayer to make Jesus your personal Lord and Savior, you gave Him the invitation and the right to live in your heart and to help you live out His will in your soul. Not only did your prayer allow Jesus to live within your spirit, but it also caused your spirit to be born again.

Now that I answered your first question about what just happened to you, let's move on to the next big questions you have: *Now what? What am I supposed to do now?* The following pages in this book will answer that question. This book is an outline of the next important steps you need to take to continue your journey with Jesus.

The prayer you prayed, along with believing in your heart, got you access to heaven when you die. The steps that follow in this book are what will help you access the *life* here on earth that Jesus wants you to live. These steps don't have to be taken in order. For example, you don't have to start attending church first and then start reading your Bible next.

You can take these steps simultaneously or all at the same time. The steps are easier when taken together because they support each other. For example, this book will encourage you to attend a church, read your Bible, and pray. When you attend church, it will encourage you to read your Bible. When you read your Bible, it will encourage you to pray. And a great way to learn how to pray is by participating at church. Do you see how these steps connect? Does it make sense? Good. Now, let's see which steps this book will cover:

1. Plug In – Attend church.
2. Shake Up – Choose the right friends.
3. Chow Down – Read your Bible.
4. TenBYTen – Pray and worship.
5. 180° – Repent (change your ways).
6. Take The Plunge – Get water baptized.
7. Draft Day – Volunteer and give.

We'll cover the details of each of these steps in each chapter. Let's start by talking about attending church. It's time to plug in.

1

PLUG IN

Attend Church Weekly.

This is not the time to pull away and neglect meeting together, as some have formed the habit of doing. In fact, we should come together even more frequently, eager to encourage and urge each other onward as we anticipate that day dawning.
Hebrews 10:25 TPT

LOW BATTERY

My family and I are huge Disney fans. We love everything Disney. We especially love taking trips to Walt Disney World; it is *the* "happiest place on earth" after all! Disney trips take a lot of planning and money. If you want a certain room at a certain resort, you must book your resort over a year in advance. Otherwise, it will probably be sold out. You must make your dining reservations months in advance to get a table where you can dine with the princesses. All this planning is even harder when you have kids to think of and plan for. You want every little detail to be as perfect as possible, and you want to capture every single memory you can.

I'll never forget one family trip we took. It was one of those magical days. Our oldest daughter had her Cinderella dress on as she marched around the park in total wonder. There, in person, were all her favorite characters! Mickey, Minnie, and even most of the princesses that she idolized were shaking her hand, giving her hugs, and waving at her. Magical music was being played throughout the park as we walked down a very clean Main Street. The smell of roasted almonds and freshly baked cookies filled the warm Orlando air. There was even a hint of turkey leg smell tempting me to buy one (you know exactly what I'm talking about if you've ever had one of their turkey legs).

We made our way down Main Street to the statue of Walt

and Mickey. On the other side of the statue, we could see the famous Cinderella Castle. It was all lit up and painted with spectacular colors. With our Mickey Mouse ice cream bars in hand, our daughter sat atop my shoulders. We made our way to the perfect spot for viewing what promised to be a spectacular firework show.

JUST LIKE YOUR SMART DEVICES NEED TO BE RECHARGED OFTEN, SO DOES YOUR SPIRIT.

Like every dad does today, I pulled out my smart phone to capture this magical moment. I got everyone in the frame, with the castle glimmering in the background. I raised up the phone and hit record. There was only one problem. My phone battery was dead. As you can imagine, this was a frustrating situation. This sort of thing has happened to all of us at one time or another; the battery on our phone is either running low or has completely died. What's the solution? Grab your charging cable and find an outlet—fast! There is nothing more satisfying than plugging in your smartphone and hearing that familiar *ding* signaling that your phone is plugged in and charging.

Have you ever been in a similar situation? Have you ever really needed your phone for something important, only to discover it either has a low battery or is completely dead? Have you missed taking a picture of an important moment? Or were you unable to call your parents when you were supposed to? Have you ever been worried you were missing an important text conversation because you couldn't turn your phone on? Have you ever been lost because you didn't have enough power to use your map app to get to your destination? Low energy is no joke, and a completely dead device is even worse. It's important to charge your devices in advance so that you don't run into these types of problems.

CHARGING

Just like your smart devices need to be recharged often, so does your spirit. While you might not be able to see, touch, or even feel your spirit; it is a very real thing. As we have already covered in this book, your spirit is the real you. Much like your body needs food to grow and remain healthy, and your mind needs information to stay sharp; your spirit needs spiritual food and exercise. Just like you need to plug in your phone to receive a charge, you need to plug in your spirit to do the same. The best way to charge up your spirit is to regularly attend church. All Christians need to do this, no matter how long they've followed Jesus. It's even more important to plug in to a local church if you're a new Christian.

"Plugging in to church" is one of those phrases Christians use. You might hear things like, "Get plugged in," or "where are you plugged in?" What people are talking about is whether you have a church you attend on a regular basis. It's important that this church is not a place you attend just every Christmas and Easter with your family. It must be a place you attend on a frequent basis, preferably every week. Just like only occasionally eating a meal won't do your body any good, attending church on special occasions won't get it done. Your attendance and involvement must be regular.

You might be asking the question: "Who came up with the idea of once-a-week church?" That's a good question. Church was originally designed to reflect how people are supposed to observe the Sabbath. The Sabbath is the holy day of the week where people are supposed to rest from their work and focus their attention on worshipping God. Today most churches meet on Sunday mornings, and some even have multiple services on Sunday. Other churches might even hold a midweek service in the evening. The point is, attend church as frequently as you can whenever they have services.

LOW-CHARGE SYMPTOMS

The symptoms of a low or dead battery on a phone can include failure to operate. The symptoms of a poorly charged spirit aren't always as obvious. Some symptoms of a spirit that needs to be recharged may include confusion, lack of life direction, hopelessness, anger, jealousy, or struggling to overcome daily temptations. If any of these symptoms are affecting you, you could probably use some time in church.

YOUTH GROUP

In addition to attending a church, it's important to find a youth group you can become part of. Youth groups are designed to share Christianity in a way that's more relatable to people your age. Most youth groups talk about common life choices that people in middle school and high school face. Youth pastors often share topics of interest to someone in your stage of life. It's not uncommon to hear messages about peer pressure, family issues, and popular culture, along with other Bible topics.

Since youth groups are designed for people your age, you'll find other people your age there. This is another reason to get involved in a youth group. You'll meet other middle and high school students who are struggling with the same things as you and are trying to find the same answers as you.

Another benefit of youth group is the style of worship at the services. Many middle and high school students sometimes don't like the style of music in the service their parents attend. That's usually not the case with youth worship teams. While worship is not about you and what you might like or dislike, it is important to find a worship style you're comfortable with and enjoy. When you like the worship music, it's easier to participate. And your participation is very important! I'll cover the reasons why in a later chapter.

Finally, youth groups often host special events in addition to their weekly services. These events will help you create new relationships and memories that will stay with you for a long time. Youth groups often have weeklong summer camps or seasonal weekend retreats. Many groups also host movie nights, worship nights, game nights, and fun social events. Church events like these can be similar to what your school may offer; but with youth group events, you'll get to hang out with people who share your faith.

If your church doesn't have services for youth, don't give up! Continue to attend church until a youth group becomes available. And if they never end up offering youth services, talk to your parents and pastor about attending a youth group elsewhere. The bottom line is to plug in! Get plugged in to church first, and if available, youth group as well.

BENEFITS, REASONS, AND CONCERNS

Going to church is not an optional thing you do in *addition* to your personal faith; it should be a major *part* of your faith. Now that you're a Jesus follower and understand the importance of plugging in, you're probably considering your church options. While you're trying to decide where to go, I want you to think about three things.

1. What are the benefits to going to church?
2. What are the main reasons for going to church?
3. What <u>concerns</u> do you have about church?

There are many <u>benefits</u> to attending church every week. We'll cover those in detail in a minute. There are also two <u>reasons</u>

why you need to attend a church every week. We'll lay those out in detail when we talk about being "planted." There are also probably some concerns you have about church; we'll cover those as well. Finally, we'll wrap up the chapter with a few things you need to look for when choosing a church.

BENEFITS

First, there are many <u>benefits</u> to attending church every week. These benefits will fix many of the symptoms that come with a low spiritual battery, like we talked about earlier. These benefits include accountability, growth, community, and worship. When I talk about church, I mean attending either the main service or the youth group. Most churches have services for the adults, and they also have different services for the youth. I strongly encourage you to attend both, if you can, because you'll get different things out of each of them.

When you attend church, you're allowing yourself to be accountable to your friends and mentors. They can support you when you need help. They can answer the questions you might have. They can challenge you when you need it. When you attend church, you position yourself for growth. The things you learn in church and the

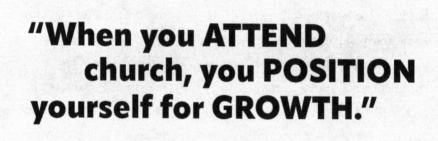

"When you ATTEND church, you POSITION yourself for GROWTH."

opportunities you get to serve will help you grow and mature as a person and as a Jesus follower.

When you attend church, you become part of a community. Much like your role in your own family, you'll become part of your church community where you'll learn how to connect with others and put the needs of others first. And when you attend church, you'll have plenty of chances to participate in worship. While you need to spend time worshipping God on your own, (more on this in Chapter Four) there is no other place on earth, other than church, that gives you the chance to worship God with other people every week.

Let's look at each benefit in more detail.

Accountability - The first benefit of attending church regularly is that you'll gain some accountability in your life. *Accountability* can be a big word for some people, so let me define it. Accountability is when someone can challenge you about something and follow up with you about doing it. You probably have experienced accountability before in your life.

Maybe your teammates hold you accountable to practicing your skills every week. Maybe they follow up with you on whether you're spending time in the weight room or conditioning. Maybe your friends hold you accountable about not hanging out with someone who always gets you into trouble. Or maybe accountability comes in the form of your parents helping make sure you get your homework done on time. The point is, none of us can do life alone, and we all need accountability from time to time in different parts of our lives.

When you attend church, you place yourself under accountability. No one said the life of a Jesus follower was easy. In fact, being a Christian can be hard sometimes. Consider the fact that you probably haven't been a Christian for very long, and it can be even harder. As you live out your newfound faith, you'll need someone to help encourage you to stay in church. You'll need someone to help motivate you to read your Bible every day. And you'll probably need someone to check in on whether you're sticking to the things Jesus asks you to commit to.

When I was a youth pastor, I had students come to me every week with news that they had "failed" in some way. If I had a dollar for every time a student told me about how they gave in to temptation, I'd be a millionaire today. Students would share how they were struggling with things like partying or pornography. They'd share how they had pushed physical boundaries with their boyfriend or girlfriend. Or they would vent about how they wanted to honor their parents but kept blowing it under pressure.

Students would share with me how they *wanted* to read their Bibles, but somehow they always put it off for time on social media or to play video games. Guys would share about their struggles with losing their tempers, while girls would share about their struggles with gossip. Do you know what a common theme was for all these young people? Often, they were trying to fight the battle on their own. Do you know what often helped them win? Accountability.

WHEREVER THERE WAS ACCOUNTABILITY, THERE WAS SUCCESS.

No matter what the scenario was, whenever they had accountability in the situation, it always improved. Let me say that again. Wherever there was accountability, there was success. Whether students partnered with their parents, a sibling, a friend, or me; accountability improved the situation. When you attend church regularly, you position yourself to be accountable to others. You'll make friends and gain mentors in church that will be there to check in on you, challenge you, and encourage you when you need it most.

Growth - Another benefit you get from attending church regularly is the growth you experience. When you attend church, you position yourself for growth. As much as you might not like going to school, not going would result in you lacking knowledge about things like reading and math. For example, while your friends would be able to read articles online, you'd still be stuck trying to get through *The Cat in the Hat!* That's embarrassing and discouraging to consider. You'd be in this position because growth happens at school, and without school, you wouldn't grow.

In school, you learn about things that are important to daily living. The reason you can solve math problems, tell what time it is, interpret the weather, and understand how our government works is because you attend school. School creates growth opportunities, and church does too. While growth in school is mostly academic, growth in church is spiritual, emotional, and social. Church, just like school, teaches you things that are important to daily living. But church also teaches you things that are important about life after we leave this planet.

Growth will occur as you sit under teaching from your pastor. When you listen to the messages your pastor teaches, it will help identify areas of your life where you need to mature. For example, your pastor might teach a lesson on what the Bible says about worrying. As your pastor shares stories about people who worry, statistics about how worry affects a person's health, and Bible verses that cover worry, you'll discover growth opportunities in your own life.

I KNOW YOU WOULDN'T ADMIT THIS TO ANYBODY, BUT YOU HAVE A STRONG DESIRE TO BELONG TO SOMETHING.

Growth from church attendance not only happens from listening to the weekly messages, but it can also happen when you are serving or volunteering. I'll discuss volunteering at church in more depth in a later chapter, but for now, know that serving your local church brings many opportunities to grow and mature in your faith. Volunteering on the traffic team during the winter reminds you what it means to sacrifice something like the comfort of a warm building. Helping in children's church reminds you that life is not all about what you want. You quickly learn about putting others' needs before your own.

Community - Along with accountability and growth, attending church brings the benefits of being part of a community. I know you wouldn't admit this to anybody, but you have a strong desire to belong to something. Every person on the planet wants to belong, and it's a secret that every person tries to hide. We all want to belong to someone or something. This is one reason why you get so depressed when you see your friends together on Instagram while you're stuck at home alone. It's what our current culture calls "fear of missing out" (a.k.a., FOMO). The fact that they didn't invite you to the party makes you feel like you don't belong, and not belonging to someone or something will crush you.

Church is another place where you can belong. When you

attend church, you become part of that community. Most youth groups will host tons of events throughout the school year and through the summer. Attending these events will bring many opportunities to hang out with people who hold similar values and are in the same season of life as you. It's a great place to create new friendships and strengthen current ones.

And even if you have a group of friends at school, you can build your community at church too! Did you know that? You can have friends at church. Did you know that all your friends don't have to come from school? When I was a youth pastor, I had some parents tell me an interesting story about their daughter. I want to share it with you in hopes that it might change how you view friendships.

Their daughter was having a birthday party, so she was told to make her list of people she wanted to invite. She attended a public school and attended youth group at church every week. When the parents got her list, they noticed something strange. Her entire list of friends was from school. She didn't list a single friend from youth group. This seemed strange to her parents as she hung out with friends from youth group all the time. When her parents asked her why she didn't invite any of her youth group friends, she said,

"I guess I didn't think even think of them. When you said *friends*, I automatically thought of my friends at school."

ONE OF THE BIGGEST FACTORS TO HOW STRONG YOUR FAITH IS, IS HOW STRONG YOUR CHRISTIAN FRIENDSHIPS ARE.

Isn't that crazy? You might find yourself in the same situation. I encourage you to change how you view friendships. If you go to public school and have friends there, *great!* It's good to have strong relationships with people at school. But if you go to youth group every week already, or if you plan to in the future, build relationships there too.

You'll meet new friends at this church community you've recently picked or have already been a part of. Just like in school or on your travel soccer team, you'll meet people at church that you click well with. The great thing is that the people you meet will do a better job of pulling you closer to your faith in Jesus than in pushing you away from it. One of the biggest factors to how strong your faith is, is how strong your Christian friendships are.

Not only will you meet new friends at church, but you'll also meet new mentors. You probably already have a mentor or two in your life. It might be your parents, a coach, or a teacher. At church, you'll find that your pastor, youth pastor, or small-group leader can become a mentor too. You'll see that these men and women care about you and want you to succeed.

They will celebrate life victories with you, and they'll help guide you when you're going through rough times. They'll will give you great advice about your faith. They'll nudge you in the right direction when you face a big decision. They'll hold you accountable when you're struggling. And they'll even challenge you when you aren't living up to your greatest potential. (More accountability!) Most importantly, they'll model Jesus for you and point you towards Him.

These mentors from your church community will also try to answer the tough questions you have about God, the Bible, and your faith. They'll teach you like your teachers do in school. They'll inspire you like your coaches do on the field. And they'll care for you in similar ways that your parents do.

Worship - The final benefit of attending church I want to share is that it provides you a place to worship. Worship may be a new idea to you. After all, you recently made this decision to live out your faith in Jesus, so let's first try to define worship, and then I will show you how church helps you experience it.

Worship is a very religious-sounding word. It can be a difficult idea to grasp because people don't worship much in modern-day life. But people worship *many* different things every day without even knowing it. People worship sports, video games, movie stars, or money. One definition for *worship* is "to regard with great or extravagant respect, honor, or devotion."[1] The Bible defines *worship* more like a way of living. In other words, the life of a Christian is worship. But there is also the *act* of worship, and that's what I'll focus on in regard to attending church.

The act of worship is often reserved for somebody important. People have been known to worship kings, other gods, and even celebrities. You might be picturing in your mind a person that is lifting their hands in the air or bowing down to someone or something. While these can be physical acts of worship, they're not all there is to worship. As a verb, *worship* means "to perform or take part in an act of worship."[1] For example, when your church plays a worship song and people sing along, they perform an act of worship because they're singing to God (or at least they should be).

Webster's dictionary defines *worship* as a verb and a noun. One noun definition of *worship* is a form of religious practice. In other words, worship would include attending church, singing a song to God, volunteering at church, donating to the church, and reading the Bible. In the simplest terms, worship is our response to God through how we live. Church gives you a place to respond; it gives you a place to worship.

It can be difficult to sing songs to God when you're in the middle of class. It's hard to focus on the Bible when you're bagging groceries at work. It's hard to pray when you're scrolling through social media. But, when you attend church, you position yourself for worship. You might be wondering why worship is important. I'll cover the importance along with what worship looks like and how to do it in a later chapter. For now, let's continue looking at getting plugged into church by covering the two reasons you should attend church.

REASONS

Let's cover two major <u>reasons</u> to attend church. People could probably list many different reasons, but to make things simple for you, I've put them into two categories. You need to attend church so that you can *give* and *receive*. That's it! Church provides you a place where you can do both. While this book has used the analogy of attending church to plugging something in, the Bible uses the analogy of a plant being planted. It says, "Those who are planted in the house of the Lord shall flourish in the courts of our God."[2]

IN THE SIMPLEST TERMS, WORSHIP IS OUR RESPONSE TO GOD THROUGH HOW WE LIVE.

Have you ever planted something before? Maybe you had that one science class where you got to plant a flower seed in a paper cup and watch the progress of its growth over the following weeks. You planted the seed in the cup, you watered it every day, and you left it on the windowsill so that the sun could do its thing. As the plant grew each day, your science teacher taught about photosynthesis while you were praying it wouldn't be on the test. If you're like me, you didn't have much success with the plant. Some of my classmates' plants grew tall and flourished, but mine would hardly grow at all.

A flourishing plant is one that grows tall, is strong, and produces much fruit. If the plant is a flower, then it produces a big, bright flower with beautiful petals. If the plant is an apple tree, then it produces a full tree of apples. Whatever the plant is, and whatever fruit it produces, one sign of a flourishing plant is *lots* of fruit. When a plant is planted in a garden by a gardener, it gets care. It gets water and food from the gardener, and it gets rain and sun from God. But a plant that flourishes not only *receives* many good things, but it also *gives* many good things.

A corn plant will give many ears of corn if it's flourishing. A blueberry bush will give many pounds of blueberries if it's flourishing. A large oak tree will give plenty of shade and protection for animals and people if it's flourishing. The Bible paints the picture of someone flowering when they're planted in church so that we'll learn the lesson of *why* we need to be in church. When we attend church, when we plug in, or when we are "planted," we *give* some things, and we *receive* some things.

Giving - In the church community, it's often said that people give of their time, talent, and tithe to the church. What does that mean? When you attend church, particularly when you volunteer at church, you're giving your time. You could spend time playing video games. You could spend time watching a basketball game. You could spend time scrolling through social media. Or you could spend time helping with the toy drive at church. When you're planted in a church, you get the chance to give your time to what Jesus is doing.

You can also give your talents to your church. Maybe you're good at singing or playing guitar. The worship team at church could use your talents. Maybe you have an eye for photography or videography. Your church could use your talent to produce material for its social-media account. Or maybe you have a great attention to detail. Your church could use your help in proofreading slides for the service.

The last thing you can give is your tithe. We'll cover tithing and giving money to church later in the book. For now, just know that every church needs money to operate. When you plug in to your local church, one thing you give is your money. Without money, churches can't pay their bills or run their programs to help their communities.

Receiving - While there are several things you give from being part of a church, there are also some things you receive. We already discussed the benefits you receive from attending church, including accountability, growth, community, and worship. In addition to these, you'll also receive several things directly from your pastor. I'll highlight three of them for you to consider.

1. You'll get spiritual leadership.
2. You'll get weekly teaching from the Bible.
3. You'll have access to pastoral care.

One thing that comes from being planted in a church is the fact that you have a front-row seat to the spiritual leadership your pastor provides. You'll discover how to be a light to the community through their example. You'll get to observe how your pastor treats people in the community and how they represent Jesus in the marketplace. You'll see what a healthy marriage and family should look like through their example. And you'll witness how your pastor leads the church members and church staff, providing you with a standard of how a Christian should lead a group of people.

THE BIBLE IS MORE THAN JUST SOME OLD BOOK.

You'll also receive weekly Bible teaching from your pastor. We've covered the importance of the Bible already, and we'll provide greater detail on daily Bible reading in a later chapter. But it's important to know that in addition to your own personal time reading the Bible, you'll also need to hear teaching from the Bible from someone who has been called to be a pastor of a church. God gives pastors special gifts and a heart to teach church members. When you combine your personal Bible reading with the teaching you get from your pastor in church, it will help you quickly and accurately understand what you read.

The Bible is more than just some old book. It's more than just a history textbook. It's more than just a collection of inspirational prayers and poems. And it's more than just a book of rules and regulations for living. While it includes all these things, it's *literally* God's words to us! It's like His love letter to us. Since the Bible is important, and since following what it says improves our lives, it's important to learn all you can from a good teacher like your pastor.

Jesus said that a person can't live only by eating food, but that person must hear the Bible too. Think about that for a second. Jesus said that to live a healthy, successful, and happy life, you must read the Bible every day. Think about your friends and family. Think about the people you go to school or work with. How many of them are miserable? How many of them are angry? How many of them are depressed or anxious? I'm pretty sure there are more of them who are than who aren't. That's pretty sad.

One of the reasons so many Christians aren't doing very well is they don't read their Bibles every day or even at all. Our society believes that the Bible is out of date and doesn't apply to our everyday lives, so they don't read it anymore. That idea couldn't be further from the truth. Here are just some of the topics the Bible covers:

- Abortion
- Alcohol

- Anger
- Anxiety
- Being a Student
- Being an Employee
- Competition
- Depression
- Drugs
- Entertainment
- Eternity
- Exercise
- Fear
- Greed
- Health Issues
- Heaven
- Hell
- Homosexuality
- Honoring Parents
- Hypocrites
- Love
- Lust
- Marriage
- Money

- Owning a Business
- Parenting
- Politics
- Pornography
- Prayer
- Relationships
- Rest
- Sickness and Disease
- Temptation
- The Poor
- The Rich
- Truth
- War
- Work

After reading this list, which *doesn't* cover *everything* in the Bible, do *you* think it is outdated or not relevant to everyday living? I trust you're gaining a better understanding of what Jesus said about the Bible when He said, "People do not live by bread alone, but by every word that comes from the mouth of God."[3]

Jesus wasn't saying that if a person doesn't read the Bible, they will physically die from starvation. But as you can see, people who do not "feed" on the Word are not experiencing the life that they could and should. Hearing the Bible is extremely important to your new faith in Jesus. The best way to hear these words is by reading the Bible for yourself, which I address in Chapter Three: Chow Down. But another way you hear is through the teaching of a pastor, and the best way to hear teaching from a pastor is by attending church. When you attend church, you hear the Bible, and when you hear the Bible, you set yourself up to win in life.

Not only will you hear the Bible being taught at church, but you'll also hear the testimonies of your peers and mentors. When you plug in to a church, you put yourself in a position to hear the triumphs and trials that your peers and mentors go through. You'll hear stories from your friends as they share how God has been good to them. You'll discover how real the Bible is as your friends share things that have happened to them because of living by what the Bible says. Your mentors will share their own testimonies as well as testimonies of others in church. Hearing these things will support what you're reading in the Bible and will boost your faith.

You'll also hear about trials that your peers and mentors have been through. You'll discover that even life with Jesus isn't perfect. You'll see that just because you became a Christian doesn't mean bad things stop happening. But you'll also hear that even in the middle of trials, God is still faithful and the Bible is still true. Hearing these things will also boost your faith.

Finally, you'll have pastoral care available to you when you need it. We all go through difficult times in life. No matter how strong your faith is or how faithful God is, life will throw you a curveball or two. The book of Psalms says, "The righteous person faces many troubles, but the Lord comes to the rescue each time."[4] One way that the Lord comes to your rescue is through your church and your pastor.

Your pastor can counsel you and pray with you when you need help. Your pastor can visit you or your family members in the hospital. Your pastor can be there at the end of the life of a family member for the funeral arrangements. Not only can your pastor provide care during trials, but they can also provide care during joyful events in life. Your pastor can be the one who dedicates a baby, baptizes you, or oversees your pre-marital counseling or wedding ceremony!

As you can see, there are some great benefits to attending church regularly. When you plug in to a local church and youth group (if available), life just gets better! And you now have a better understanding of the two main reasons *why* you need to attend church. When you get planted in a local church, you position yourself to flourish where you can both give and receive.

ONE WAY THAT THE LORD COMES TO YOUR RESCUE IS THROUGH YOUR CHURCH AND YOUR PASTOR.

But you may still have some concerns. People can be nervous about attending church, especially if they have never been to church before or if they're new in their faith. Let's look at some of the more common concerns and try to encourage you.

CONCERNS

As I already said, some people are nervous about going to church. You might be one of those people. Church is unlike any other place you might visit. When you're at home, everyone there knows everything about you. Home is a place where you can wear your pajamas and not worry about having to look your best. Home is where you relax and even let people see the uglier sides of your personality. It's where you tend to show your laziness and grumpiness; but you aren't as bold to show these characteristics at school, work, or the store.

When you're at school, you tend to show your best side. You try to act like you have it all together. Most people try to look their best at school, but they also try to act like somebody they're not. Most people want their classmates to see the best version of themselves, kind of like what people put on their social media accounts. We want to appear like we're in control and successful. And it's kind of ironic that people care so much about what others think at school. School isn't a religious place where everyone agrees on what's right and wrong. So while people may still be judgmental at school, there isn't as much shame about making bad choices.

Other places like the movie theater or the mall aren't that important because you usually don't know anybody there. I call this the Walmart effect. Have you been to Walmart lately? If you haven't, you need to check it out. It's as if people who go shopping at that store have completely given up on what's considered socially acceptable. This is where people go out in public wearing things that should embarrass them, but it doesn't. The reason people show up in tank tops, yoga pants, and fuzzy boots is because they figure no one will know them at Walmart. (Not that I'm judging if this describes YOU). And if no one knows them, they don't care about how they look. There's no reason to put their best self out there, and there's no reason to care if they're judged.

BEING JUDGED HASN'T BEEN A PROBLEM FOR YOU BEFORE, SO IT SHOULDN'T BE A PROBLEM FOR YOU IN ATTENDING CHURCH.

As I said before, church, on the other hand, is unique. Church is a place where people go to put on their best side. It's a place to go where many people know you well. And it's a place where there can be some judgement because of the high moral standard that's expected. Because of these reasons, along with others, you may have the following concerns:

1.   You're concerned people will judge you.

2.   You're concerned it will be boring.

3.   You're concerned people will be weird.

You're Concerned People Will Judge You - Let's get this concern addressed with a dose of reality. Yes, somebody might judge you. But people judge you all the time anyway, and that might not have stopped you before. Think about it. You might have tried out for the school talent show knowing that you were going to be judged. You might have tried out for the soccer team knowing that the coach was going to judge you. You may have dated that guy knowing your friends were going to judge you. There was probably a time when you pierced something, changed your hair color, or wore something strange. Guess what? People judged you then. Being judged hasn't been a problem for you before, so it shouldn't be a problem for you in attending church.

Second, you'll find that *most* people at church and youth group *won't* judge you because they were once in your shoes. The Bible says that we have *all* sinned. Every person that attends church or youth group is dealing with something. We all have a past; some of us even have a present. We are all struggling and need God's grace.

So, when you finally decide to attend church, you'll find most people are excited to have you and want to help you with your journey.

You're Concerned It Will Be Boring - Another dose of reality here. You're right; it might be boring. It might be just like some of your classes at school: some are boring, and some classes are fun. You may experience a church or youth group that's boring. But you can also find one that is fun that you'll enjoy! You won't know until you go. You must get plugged in to discover what a place is like. If you find it's not engaging or feeding you, then try another place. But I want to encourage you to give it some time and effort first. Try it out for a few months, and see what happens.

The reason you might have to give it some time first is because what we often label as "boring" is just something we don't understand yet. The more you learn about something, the more interested in it you become. Let me give you an example of this with a story about my wife, Mia.

Mia teaches piano to kids of all ages. She is an *amazing* teacher, the best I know. Mia makes learning fun. She not only teaches kids about piano and music, but she also plays games that help strengthen the lessons. Most kids are enrolled in piano lessons by their parents. The kids might not want to learn piano, but the parents want them to learn it.

So, for many kids, the first few lessons aren't very exciting. But after the kids start to learn more about how to read music, identify keys, and play notes; they find it more interesting. Mia has had dozens of parents over the years tell her how their child was bored with piano lessons at first, but later they would beg their parents to keep the lessons going. Once they understood the piano, it wasn't boring anymore.

I WANT YOU TO IMAGINE THE WORST-CASE SCENARIO.

You're Concerned People Will Be Weird - Let's talk about one of my favorite topics. Seriously, I *love* talking about weird church people. Let's be honest; weird church people exist. That's a valid concern, so let's talk about it for a moment, shall we? I want you to imagine the worst-case scenario. Picture the following in your mind:

> *You show up to the event, and people are dressed weird. They're all wearing the same colors, almost like they are on the same team. Some of the people have painted their faces; some men have even painted their chests. Some of them are wearing wigs, masks, and costumes. They don't just show up on time for the event, they show up hours early. Some are at the event even before the sun rises.*

> *They all park their cars in the parking lot and set up lawn chairs around the cars. They get their grills out and start grilling all kinds of meat. Coolers are stocked full of drinks, and people are even flying flags. They've got their stereos cranked up; they're blasting music and dancing. These people are hanging out and eating together, in a parking lot, hours before the doors even open.*

> *Once inside, the energy in the place is amazing. To say that the venue is noisy is an understatement. A band plays music leading up to the event, a DJ plays popular songs over the sound system. Thousands of people at the event sing out loud together as their favorite songs and chants are played. People are screaming, literally screaming, things like, "Score! Come on, Man! Get him!" And when something during the event goes*

their way, people scream at the top of their lungs and high-five everyone around them.

Sounds like a crazy intense scene, doesn't it? Sounds like these people are not only weird; they're fanatics!

The scenario I just had you imagine is something that happens at sporting events across the country every single week. From high-school games to college playoffs, this weirdness is on full display. This is what things look like in professional sports, and they're broadcasting it on national television for all to see.

It doesn't matter if it's a soccer match in Europe, a Friday-night-football game at your local high school, or a Major League Baseball game on TV; people act like complete fools to support their favorite team or player. And let me say, I am just as guilty of it as anyone!

You don't have to worry about people being any weirder in church than any other place. If that's what's keeping you from going to church, why doesn't it keep you from attending a concert or major sporting event? If you're willing to go to those with no issues but you aren't willing to go to church, then you're fooling yourself.

That being said, let's be honest; there are some weirdos at church too. I call these people "granola" because they act like fruits, nuts, and flakes. (See what I did there?) If you're expecting everyone in church to be normal, it's time to lower your expectations. There are weird people in church just like there are weird people in your school. I want to encourage you to be aware of this going in, so you can cut people some slack and not be shocked.

IF YOU'RE WILLING TO GO TO THOSE WITH NO ISSUES BUT YOU AREN'T WILLING TO GO TO CHURCH, THEN YOU'RE FOOLING YOURSELF.

We're all a work in progress. The bottom line is that if worrying about people being weird is holding you back, then don't worry. If people can act like fools because a football player carried a football from one end of the field to other, they can certainly act like fools for Jesus, the one who saved them from an eternity in hell.

All right, I think we covered all the concerns. Are you good? Great! Let's move on to the church shopping list.

SHOPPING LIST

There are literally thousands of churches across the country. Many experts estimate there are almost 400,000 churches in America. With that many places to try, choosing the right church can be overwhelming. But you must get past your reluctance so that you can find the right fit for you to plug-in. Not only are there tons of churches across the country, there are tons of *types* of churches. They all have differences in Bible teaching, worship style, ministries offered, and membership size.

Some churches are categorized as megachurches where over 500 people attend regularly. Some churches can even reach attendance in the thousands. There are also smaller churches, those with less than 500 people attending regularly. Most experts agree that the average church in America has around 100-150 people in weekly attendance.

Some churches provide a more traditional style of service. You might find pews for seating, worship songs from hymnals, and a more reserved atmosphere. While other churches might provide a more modern style where it wouldn't be out of the ordinary to see a theatrical stage design with concert-style lights, rows of chairs replacing pews, the worship set more closely resembling a concert, Bible scriptures provided on projection screens, and lots of multimedia elements.

The types of ministries offered can vary from church to church as well. Some churches have energetic kids' and youth ministries with large student bodies, while other churches' ministries for kids and students are more like small groups. Some churches focus heavily on local community outreach providing things like groceries to those in need. While other churches might focus on world missions with frequent trips oversees.

Even though you're deciding among different Christian churches to attend, keep in mind that even what they teach from the Bible can vary. Teaching from the Bible is called doctrine; it's basically the ideas and truths that come from it. Some churches are considered reformed while others are considered charismatic. From the baptism of Holy Spirit to End Times interpretation, churches could teach the same topic from different viewpoints.

It's important for you to weigh all these things as you look for which church would be the right fit for you. In other words, it's important for you to discover a place that you're comfortable with.

Comfort Level - As I mentioned before, there are several things to consider when shopping for the right church. Attendance, teaching, worship style, and the ministries they offer are all things to consider. Each of these things plays into what your comfort level is for any given location. For example, if the music isn't lively enough for you, it can distract from your worship experience. If the church doesn't have a youth group, you'll miss out on some of the things that I've already discussed you need from church.

If you find yourself not enjoying your church experience, try talking to the pastor first. See if you need to just make some adjustments in your heart and be a little more open-minded. Maybe you're just being judgmental or haven't given the church a chance. But if after giving it a chance, checking your heart, and spending time seeking God, you still aren't comfortable, you may need to look elsewhere.

The key to finding your comfort level is praying about

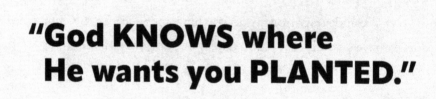

your church choices. Remember, God knows where He wants you planted. If you seek Him, He will show you where to go. The Bible says, "Seek his will in all you do, and he will show you which path to take."[5] He won't send you to the wrong place accidentally; God knows what He's doing. He will place you in the church where you'll thrive. He knows what church you need to be planted in so that you can flourish like that plant I talked about. He'll plug you in to a place where you can *give* and *receive* in amazing ways.

Friends - It's extremely important to find a church that your friends go to. It helps to go to church with people who are in the same season of life as you. This means people who are in the same grade or are the same age and have a similar family situation as you. In the next chapter, I'll discuss the importance of having the right friends with you in your newfound faith. For now, think of it this way.

It's your sixteenth birthday, and your parents have planned a surprise party for you. You pull into the driveway and can tell something is up. There are more cars on your street than normal. All the lights are off in your house. The house is completely quiet as you walk in, which is odd because the TV is usually on. You see a randomly placed streamer that has fallen on the kitchen floor. As you and your mom round the corner, you can tell she is both excited and nervous. It *is* your birthday after all. You have a feeling you know what's coming.

As you walk into the living room, you hear a collective, "Surprise!" Everyone was waiting for you. They're all dressed up and excited to see you there. There is just one problem. You don't recognize *anybody*, not one person! There's a newborn baby crying in some lady's arms. There's an elderly couple who are old enough to be your grandparents, but it's not your grandparents. And even though there are about a dozen people your age in the group, you've never met any of them before in your life. And the strangest part is, they don't know you either.

It's your birthday. It's a special moment in your life. It's the type of event you want to spend with the people you're closest to. Church can and should be the same way. You want to experience all the memories and life change that will happen at church with people you're close to. So, even if it's just one person, try to attend somewhere that includes some of your friends. Oftentimes you'll commit to Jesus because someone you know brought you to church. So you may have already found the church that fits your comfort level that your friends attend. If not, ask around. Find out where your friends are attending, and if you get the chance, check out that church too.

WHEN CHURCH IS "AROUND THE CORNER," IT'S HARDER FOR YOUR DRIVER TO SAY NO.

Close to Home - The last item on your church shopping list is to find a place that's close to home. There are several reasons this one's important, all of which I experienced when I was a youth pastor. I'll cover as many as I can to finish up this chapter.

Finding a church close to home is important, especially if you and your parents don't share the same faith. I understand that most of you reading this book will probably attend church *with* your family. But when I was pastoring, I had several students attend our church or youth group whose parents didn't.

Maybe you got saved at a youth camp or during a youth

service, and your parents weren't there. Maybe your parents work on Sundays. Maybe your parents are hostile to church and don't want to have anything to do with it. Whatever the family situation might be, it's good to have a church close to home in the event your parents are just dropping you off to church.

You don't want your transportation to have any excuse for not taking you to service If you're hitching a ride to church every week. Attending a church far away from home increases the likelihood of this happening. When church is "around the corner," it's harder for your driver to say no.

Another reason to find a church that's close to home is because of the hectic schedules people have these days. Many students are involved in extracurricular activities or sports at school. Maybe you have band practice or a soccer scrimmage the same night of the week the youth group meets. Or maybe you have a cheer tournament after church Sunday or will be on the road early Sunday morning for a baseball tournament. No matter what you have going on, you don't want to let it get in the way of plugging in.

It's a lot easier to finish up your basketball practice, get changed, grab dinner, and head to youth group on a Wednesday night when service is around the corner. It makes it nearly impossible to get involved in church with that type of schedule when you live an hour away.

The last reason to consider when measuring the distance between home and church is the weather. I understand this might not apply to people all around the country, but I live in Michigan in the heart of the Midwest. We experience very hostile winters! It's not unusual to get a couple feet of snow one night or an ice storm over the weekend. These types of weather events can make roads dangerous. These circumstances often discourage parents and guardians from venturing out, let alone allowing you to venture out if you can drive.

When you cut down the distance from home or school to church, it reduces the risk that bad weather can play in preventing you from attending service. Side note: I would never encourage you to endanger your life for any reason, including going to church. Always follow the advice of your parents and authorities when it comes to bad weather. This is just another thing to think about when considering where to attend church.

In bringing this topic to a close, let me address the elephant in the room. You might be reading about the importance of getting plugged in while thinking to yourself, "Can't I just watch church online?" That's a great point. In fact, watching church online would address many of the things I covered in your shopping list.

Churches across the country experienced a massive increase in online streaming and attendance during the COVID-19 pandemic of 2020. As a result of lockdowns and social-distancing measures, many people stayed home to watch church online. While there are benefits to being able to watch services online (re-watching a service for review or catching the on-demand video if you couldn't attend in person), there are also some downsides. The most obvious disadvantage is that you won't get any face-to-face interaction with other people. It's also more difficult to volunteer if you're just watching a service streamed online. To summarize, use online service as an alternative if you must, but don't make it a substitute for in-person church attendance. Get plugged in.

2

SHAKE UP

Choose the right friends.

Do not be misled: "Bad company corrupts good character."
1 Corinthians 15:33 NIV

Let me tell you a quick story about a cool nature place where my wife, Mia, and I have taken our kids. During the summer in Michigan, we make it a priority to get outside as much as possible. Remember how I talked about the brutal winters? With almost six months of cloudy days throughout the year, enjoying the sun and fresh air from June through August in Michigan is a must. One way we take advantage of this is by taking the kids to the Kalamazoo Nature Center (KNC).

The KNC has a ton of things for kids to do outside. They can walk on trails, visit the Kalamazoo River, play on a natural playground, and visit the KNC Museum. There are tons of wildlife present and plenty of activities to experience. One of the experiences available is the Butterfly Garden. It's a beautiful area full of dozens of wildflowers and plants that attract butterflies. I have never seen so many butterflies in one place as I have in the Butterfly Garden. It's such a popular destination that weddings are often held there.

Butterflies of every shape, size, and color hang out on plants and fly around your head. It's incredible to see how our kids respond to the beauty and detail that God has provided in the wings of those little creatures. They'll watch as the butterflies float around their heads, and they'll try their hardest to get one to land on their hand or arm. There is something about butterflies that shows beauty in a way few creatures can.

There is one thing, however, that you won't see in the

Butterfly Garden. As you watch these winged creatures flutter around the garden, no matter how hard you look for them, you won't find any caterpillars. You won't see any caterpillars climbing around the plants that the butterflies are on. Why is that the case? Because caterpillars and butterflies don't hang out with each other.

You might be thinking to yourself, "Well, that's kind of rude! Are butterflies too good to hang out with caterpillars?" Not necessarily. I'm pretty sure caterpillars don't even think about butterflies. I suppose if caterpillars had an Instagram account, they might scroll through their feed envying all the butterfly posts, but they don't. The real reason they don't hang out with each other is because they're two distinctly different types of creatures. They live completely different lives with different sets of goals, characteristics, and habits.

For example, butterflies fly high above the ground. They soar from plant to plant in no time at all. Caterpillars, on the other hand, crawl around on the ground. In fact, they don't just crawl, they crawl *slowly*. It takes caterpillars far more time to get from point A to point B than it does a butterfly. Even if caterpillars manage to get up off the ground to climb around on plants or trees, it takes *forever* in comparison to butterflies.

Another difference between butterflies and caterpillars is their appearance. Butterflies have wings that are painted beautifully with colors and patterns, much like art you would find in a museum. Caterpillars may be colorful, but they aren't considered beautiful. Most caterpillars feel weird to the touch. They have strange things sticking out of their backs, and sometimes they look like they are covered in hair. If you think I'm out of line with my assessment, think about this for a second. Have you ever known anybody who collects caterpillars? Not likely. But people collect butterflies all the time.

BECAUSE CATERPILLARS AND BUTTERFLIES DON'T HANG OUT WITH EACH OTHER.

Consider the differences in the diet of these two creatures. Butterflies mainly eat liquids. Much like a hummingbird, butterflies live off nectar from flowers. Caterpillars don't drink liquids. They munch on the leaves of plants. Search hard enough, and I'm sure you could find a leaf in your backyard that looks like Swiss cheese—full of nibbled holes. I could go on about the differences, but the point is that these two creatures couldn't be any more different from each other. It makes sense that these two don't really have lots of opportunities or reasons to hang out with each other.

With all these differences in mind, the fascinating thing to think about is that butterflies were once caterpillars. Isn't that crazy? To put it another way, caterpillars are destined to turn into butterflies! Most of us learned in science that caterpillars go through a process called metamorphosis where they literally change from one type of creature into another. Caterpillars become butterflies, and butterflies used to be caterpillars!

You can learn a lot from these creatures and the process of metamorphosis as a new Christian. It's almost like God placed this process in nature to teach us some lessons. Among those lessons is the idea that we don't have to remain stuck in our current ways. We can learn and grow in our character and behaviors. As we mature in our faith, we can see personal improvements in our lives. We also don't have to settle for the same results we've been getting. With hard work, faith in God, and an attitude of not giving up, we can do almost anything!

WE CAN LEARN AND GROW IN OUR CHARACTER AND BEHAVIORS.

SHAKE UP

When you follow butterflies and caterpillars, you also learn that creatures in nature tend to hang out with their own kind. Now, before I continue this idea, let me address something first. The idea of hanging out with your own kind has produced some evil ideas, things like racism, the history of global slavery, and what happened to the Jewish people in World War II are all the result of people twisting ideas like this.

By no means does hanging out with your "kind" mean judging people by their skin color or economic status. I'm using the illustration of two distinct types of creatures in nature to land the point that there are benefits to regularly interacting with people who share your values and belief system. In other words, before you were a Christian, you might have hung out with people who were hostile or uncaring to Christianity, but now that you are a Christian, it's important to spend time with people who embrace the Christian faith.

Let me put this another way. You used to be a caterpillar, and now you're a butterfly. While the caterpillar experienced metamorphosis in a cocoon to become a butterfly, you experienced being born again to become a Christian. Now that you've had such a radical change in your life, one of the important steps to take is to radically change some of your friends. It's time to shake things up!

I know that everyone who reads this book is in a different position. You may be reading this book thinking you don't have to shake things up with your relationships. Maybe you have always hung out with Christians; in fact, they're the ones who invited you to church where you made Jesus the Lord and Savior of your life. Or you could have a group of friends who pretty much stay out of trouble and are a positive influence on you. Or you may be reading this book thinking you have a lot of work to do with your relationships. Maybe the people you hang out with curse like sailors and get drunk on the weekends. Whatever your position, I want you to be honest with yourself and with God about your situation. Take a survey of who you have in your life. And if this chapter encourages you to make some changes, make the changes. You'll be better off for it.

I'll be honest with you. This is a frequent topic I teach on. I have spoken to youth all across the country over the last decade about choosing friends wisely. The decision to end toxic friendships is one I find students struggle with the most. I get it. Your friends are your whole world right now. They often determine what classes you sign up for and what you plan on doing Saturday night. But the truth is, Jesus should be your whole world, and when He is, it will cause you to shake things up.

METAMORPHOSIS

The apostle Paul once wrote, "This means that anyone who belongs to Christ has become a new person. The old life is gone; a new life has begun!"[1] In fact, this Bible verse uses the same word we use when we talk about the process of a caterpillar becoming a butterfly. The word that is used is *metamorphoo*. It sounds weird because it's Greek, but it also might sound a little familiar to you. If it does, it's because that Greek word is where we get the English word *metamorphosis*.

What Paul is saying is that when you became a Christian, you experienced a metamorphosis. You literally became a new person (or creature) when you were born again! And since you became a new creature, much like the caterpillar did when it became a butterfly, you should look and act differently. Do me a favor, and stop reading for a second. Put the book down, get up, walk over to a mirror, and look at yourself. When you're done, come back and pick up where you left off. I'll wait.

How was it? Did you see it? Did you see the new creature in the mirror? Probably not. You probably didn't see anything different in your appearance now that you're a Christian. Maybe you saw that you needed to comb your hair and brush your teeth, but that's about it! I'm sure you didn't *see* a new creature because when you got saved, nothing changed in you physically. All the changes took place in your spirit which you can't see with your eyes.

When you pray the prayer to make Jesus your personal Lord and Savior, nothing really changes on the outside, at least not with your body. Your behaviors and character will change over time, and I'll detail that in a minute. Remember how you're a three-part being? The "real you" is a spirit, and that spirit lives in your physical body. Your spirit is what was born again. Your spirit is what experienced metamorphosis. While you should look and act differently as a Christian, many of those changes will take time; they don't happen overnight. The spiritual change happens immediately, but the changes in how you act will happen gradually.

WHILE YOU SHOULD LOOK AND ACT DIFFERENTLY AS A CHRISTIAN, MANY OF THOSE CHANGES WILL TAKE TIME; THEY DON'T HAPPEN OVERNIGHT.

Even though these changes in your character and behavior change gradually, it's important to know what to look for. This way you can measure you progress along the way. After all, you'll want to know if you're still acting like a caterpillar. So how *should* you look and act differently? What should a "butterfly" look like? There are lots of ways you should start looking like a "butterfly," and the characteristics and behaviors that need to change will be different for everyone. But here are some common and basic ways that most people will need to change.

THE BUTTERFLY PROFILE

You might need to change the way you talk. Butterflies don't speak negatively about things. They don't complain. They don't gossip. They don't lie. They don't swear. Butterflies say things that are positive. They encourage others and speak kindly about others. They're honest with people in a kind and loving way.

Butterflies don't watch the same things that caterpillars watch. A butterfly doesn't watch horror movies or movies with a bunch of sex and nudity in them. Butterflies don't listen to depressing music or gangster rap. They don't have songs on their playlists that curse God or glorify drug use. They don't listen to things that treat women like objects.

Butterflies don't read books about magic, witches, and wizards. They don't read things about demons. Butterflies avoid pornography in all forms, not just the well-known websites but also the social media accounts that are tempting as well. Butterflies pay attention to what they put in their bodies. They're very selective about what they consume. Butterflies don't get drunk or do drugs. They don't do anything that would keep them from thinking clearly and making wise choices.

Butterflies are respectful to their parents. They honor their parents or guardians. They appreciate them for what they do and how they provide food, a home, and nice things. They're grateful to their parents or guardians for the sacrifices they make. And since they honor them, they speak kindly and respectfully to them.

I think you're starting to get the picture on ways you can work on living and acting differently. I encourage you not to put too much pressure on yourself to make all these changes happen immediately. Remember, they'll take time. And don't try to do them all on your own because you won't be able to. You'll need Jesus' help.

Remember, trying to live life on your own is how you got into your mess in the first place. Living life on your own means *you're* the lord of your life. But you decided to follow Jesus, and now *He* is the Lord of your life. *Lord* means leader, so let Him lead! The Bible says, "My old self has been crucified with Christ. It is no longer I who live, but Christ lives in me. So I live in this earthly body by trusting in the

Son of God, who loved me and gave himself for me."[2]

Don't get discouraged if you make a mistake or a bad decision. That's why God's grace is there to help you. Now that you're a Christian, Jesus can speak more clearly to your heart and help guide you in the right direction. And if you do choose the wrong path, He will help you get back on track. We'll cover this process of failing and trying again in the 180° chapter.

REMEMBER, TRYING TO LIVE LIFE ON YOUR OWN IS HOW YOU GOT INTO THIS MESS IN THE FIRST PLACE.

The way you look and act should start looking differently now that the old you died and you're born again. One way to get started with these changes is to change your influences in life. And one of the greatest influences in your life are your friends. Remember, butterflies don't hang out with caterpillars. You need to figure out who the caterpillars are in your life. It's time to shake up your relationships. Let's dig a little deeper into what that looks like.

SHOW ME YOUR FRIENDS

There's a saying that goes, "Show me your friends, and I'll show you your future." It's the idea that the quality of your life is directly connected with the type of people you choose to hang out with. The Bible says it this way: "Walk with the wise and become wise; associate with fools and get in trouble."[3] Many of us ended up in a bad spot in life because of the people we were hanging with. Have you ever noticed how you would often get in trouble when you hung out with certain people? Now that you have decided to make Jesus the Lord of your life, you need to stop hanging out with those types of people.

Let me give you a dose of reality. Your friends will either pull you closer to God or push you further away from Him. I'll say it again, so it sinks in. Your friends will either pull you closer to God or push you further away from Him. There is no middle ground. There is no in-between. Consider the relationships you have in your life right now. In your mind, go through the list of friends you have. As you think about each one, consider whether they challenge you to be a better Christian or tempt you to deny your faith.

In fact, now might be a good time to do a little exercise. No,

I'm not asking you to go for a run. Take your mental list, and write it down on a piece of paper. Make two columns on the paper, and title one column "Pull Close" and the other column "Push Away." In the "Pull Close" column, list any friends you have that pull you closer to God. For example, these are the people who invite you to church, pray with you, and hold you accountable.

In the "Push Away" column, list any friends who mock your faith. List those who tease you about your beliefs. List those who keep inviting you to do things you shouldn't like smoking, drinking, or gossiping. This list could even include a partner who keeps asking you to push the boundaries with them physically. Got your list? Good!

YOUR FRIENDS WILL EITHER PULL YOU CLOSER TO GOD OR PUSH YOU FURTHER AWAY FROM HIM.

Here is what I want you to do next. Stop reading again for a minute, and put the book down. Pick up your list and pray about it.

Ask God to help you strengthen your friendships with the people in the "Pull Close" column. Ask Him to give you courage to be honest with those in the "Push Away" column, and even to end those relationships if necessary. Once you've finished praying over your lists, pick the book back up and continue.

Now that you have spent some time praying over your lists, I believe that God will work on your heart and show you how to take this important step of shaking up your friendships. Remember, you aren't going to do this on your own. You need His help and direction. He is faithful! He *will* help! Along with praying about this step, I want to give you some things to look for in choosing the right kinds of friends. So, let's give you another shopping list like we did for choosing the right church. This shopping list is short.

SHOPPING LIST

There are only two items to consider in your search for friendships that strengthen you. Choose people who live their faith and share their faith. That's it! It's a simple list, and it's easy to identify these kinds of people. Let's review both of these shopping-list items in detail.

LIVE THEIR FAITH

The first item on your shopping list is to consider people who live their faith. By no means do these people have to be perfect. Remember, no one is perfect but Jesus. Everyone makes mistakes and bad choices. What's important is how the person responds to their failures. If they just embrace them and don't attempt to make any changes, then they're not truly living their faith.

CHOOSE PEOPLE WHO LIVE THEIR FAITH AND SHARE THEIR FAITH.

People who feel sorry for failing to live up to their faith and make changes are the types of people you're looking to befriend. Regardless of their failures and bad choices, they should show some fruit in how they live their lives for Jesus. Jesus said, "You can identify them by their fruit, that is, by the way they act. Can you pick grapes from thornbushes, or figs from thistles?"[4] Jesus used the analogy of a plant or tree to teach this idea of fruit. Let's look at another way to help you understand.

October in Michigan is a special time for Michiganders. People love seeing the weather and nature change from hot and humid to a little cooler. The trees start turning in October, and they display a wide range of beautiful colors from red and orange to purple. Apples are in season and ready to pick during this time, and with this change in nature, people become *obsessed* with apples. They drink apple lattes and apple cider. They buy apple-scented candles and eat apple-flavored donuts. And, of course, people *love* to go apple picking.

IN THE SAME WAY, CHRISTIANS SHOULD BE KNOWN FOR THE FRUIT THEY PRODUCE IN THEIR LIVES.

Apple picking is a tradition for our family too. Mia and I gather up the girls and head to the nearest orchard to fill bags full of apples. The girls love seeing if they can reach the branches on their own, and they love seeing how many apples they can get to fill their own bag. We use those apples to make applesauce and pie filling for apple pies. I bet you can smell the apples right now!

Now imagine that our family arrived home from our trip and began taking the apples out of the bags, only to discover we had bags full of oranges. That would be weird, frustrating, and impossible! It would be weird because no one has ever picked oranges from an apples tree before. It would be frustrating because our plan was to pick apples, not oranges. And it would be impossible because the only way to pick oranges is to pick them from orange trees.

The climate in Michigan is not sufficient for growing orange trees, so our family would probably have to fly to Florida to find any. This is what Jesus was trying to teach people when He talked about the type of fruit a tree produces. While apple trees are known for their apples, orange trees are known for their oranges. In the same way, Christians should be known for the fruit they produce in their lives.

You might be wondering how you "produce fruit." Do Christians start growing apples or oranges on their arms and legs? Of course not! The fruit that Jesus was talking about were behaviors and characteristics. He was explaining the same idea you were just reading about with the caterpillars and butterflies.

There is a verse in Galatians that clarifies what Jesus meant. It says, "But the Holy Spirit produces this kind of fruit in our lives: love, joy, peace, patience, kindness, goodness, faithfulness, gentleness, and self-control. There is no law against these things!"[5] What Jesus means, and what you should look for in yourself and other Christians, are these characteristics or behaviors. These things listed in Galatians are the "fruit" of the "tree" of a Christian.

In other words, as you look for people who live their faith, as you watch the type of fruit they have in their lives, it should include these things that are listed in Galatians. To help you identify these fruits, let me list some practical things you can look for.

Friends Who Attend Church - First, look for people who attend church and/or youth group regularly. If someone claims to be a Christian but never goes to church, are they really a Christian? No person knows what's in another person's heart but Jesus. And attending church is not what defines a person as a Christian. Making Jesus the Lord of your life is what makes you a Christian. But if a professional basketball player isn't on a team in the NBA, and they never play basketball, are they really a professional basketball player?

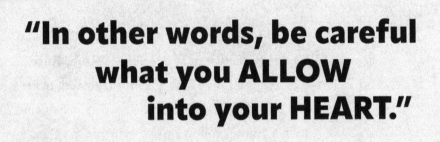

"In other words, be careful what you ALLOW into your HEART."

Look for people who love church. They love attending church and being in service. Find people who enjoy listening to the messages that are taught at church and who try to attend the events the church hosts. Look for people who don't mind sacrificing a week of their summer vacation to go to youth camp. Find people who will skip the Friday night party to attend the worship night the youth group put on instead. Bottom line, if they don't attend church regularly, or if they're not plugged in, consider finding someone else, at least until they change.

Friends Who Are Selective in What They Watch, Read, Hear, and Follow - Another thing to look for in whether someone is living their faith is how selective they are about what they watch and read. You could include who they follow on social media too. The Bible reminds you as a Jesus follower to, "Guard your heart above all else, for it determines the course of your life."[6] In other words, be careful what you allow into your heart. Christians should guard their ears and eyes because those are the entry points to their hearts. What you watch and listen to will influence you.

As you look for people to become friends with, consider the types of shows they stream. Do they watch a lot of shows with blood, and gore? Do they like watching horror movies because they like being scared? Are they caught up in shows with magic and witchcraft? While it may be difficult to cut out all forms of TV and movies, your friends should show they're selective in what they allow in their hearts. Again, no one will be perfect, but they certainly shouldn't binge on things that are against what the Bible teaches.

WHAT YOU WATCH AND LISTEN TO WILL INFLUENCE YOU.

Along with choosing friends who are selective in what they watch, pay attention to the type of music they listen to as well. While some Christians, churches, and denominations choose not to listen to secular music at all, I personally don't go that far. Secular music is any music that is not considered Christian, gospel, or worship. I personally won't suggest that you and your friends don't listen to anything secular; that is between you and God and your parents. There is a lot of great secular music out there that won't negatively influence your heart. But I do encourage you to pay close attention and filter out any harmful music.

One of the best ways to filter out music that would distract from you living your life based on the Bible is to look up the lyrics. It's a common excuse I often heard from students as a youth pastor. Students constantly told me that they don't listen to a song for the words; they just like the rhythm or the beat of the song. What those students don't know is that I wasn't born yesterday. I was once a student, and I learned firsthand how the words in music can influence a person no matter how cool the music was.

WOULD JESUS BE COMFORTABLE WITH IT IF HE WERE SITTING IN THE ROOM WITH THEM?

I listened to all genres of music when I was in high school. I listened to some Alternative music like Pearl Jam and Nirvana. I also liked some pop artists like U2 and Dave Matthews Band. And I also listened to a lot of rap music. Back then Tupac Shakur (2Pac), Snoop Dogg, and The Notorious B.I.G. (Biggie Smalls) were popular, and

I had several of their CDs. Growing up, I was a dedicated Christian
. . . until I hit high school. It was in high school that I found myself
getting drunk on the weekends, getting high after school, and looking
at pornography regularly.

I'm not saying that *just because* I listened to that kind of music,
it made me do all those things that go against my Christian faith. But
that music didn't help. We are what we eat, and there are many ways
we "feed" ourselves. We feed our bodies by eating food, we feed our
spirits by reading the Bible, and we feed our souls (mind, will, and
emotions) by what we read, watch, and listen to. Words from songs
that you and your friends listen to will get into your soul, and they *will*
influence how you think and what you believe. I've looked up lyrics
to those songs I used to listen to in high school, and now when I read
them, I'm embarrassed, offended, and not at all surprised I ended up
where I did back then.

When it comes to what kind of media your friends consume,
consider this: would Jesus be comfortable with it if He were sitting
in the room with them? It's a great question to ask of yourself
regarding what you consume too. If the answer to that question is *no*,
then it needs to be turned off or put down because Jesus *is* sitting in

that room with you—He lives in our hearts as Christians. He's always with us.

Also consider who your friends follow on social media. Social media is another form of media and another thing that our souls can consume. The statistics on how much influence social media has over people is startling. Social media contributes to all kinds of identity confusion, anxiety, and depression. However, there are some benefits to social media too. One of the greatest benefits of social media is how it connects people. Social media is also full of positive influencers, like Jesus-centered celebrities and personalities.

If your friends are following accounts that mock God and Christianity or that promote immorality in any form, you might want to reconsider building on those relationships. Build friendships with people who follow social media accounts that have a positive influence on the world, that promote the Gospel of Jesus Christ, and that challenge them to grow in their faith.

Friends Who Serve and Give - The next thing to consider when selecting your friends is whether they serve and give at church. I already talked about finding people who attend church regularly.

Also, find people who volunteer at church and financially support it. I covered the importance of serving and giving in detail in the first chapter, so I trust you get it by now. Find those who are active in this part of their faith. This way you can challenge each other in it and hold each other accountable.

WE LIVE IN A CULTURE THAT IS FOCUSED ON SELF.

People who serve and give at church are showing some spiritual maturity and a desired character trait to have in a friend. Those who serve and give understand sacrifice, and they know how to put others first. Those who serve and give tend to be less selfish, and that's something you want in a friend.

Have you ever had a friend who was all about themselves? They always wanted to talk about what they were going through but rarely listened to what you were facing? Ever had a friend who never wanted to do what you wanted to do? Have you ever been in a one-sided friendship? Were you the one who always initiated conversations and get-togethers? Were you the one sending all the texts? Did you make all the plans? Did you always invite them to things, but they rarely invited you to anything?

We live in a culture that is focused on self. Most people believe that they're the center of the universe and that everything is about them and how they feel. The last thing you need is another friend who believes and acts this way. When you find friends who give much of their personal time to helping the local church, you'll meet people who run counter to the culture and who will support you in your new faith.

IT'S IMPORTANT TO HAVE FRIENDS WHO ARE NOT SPIRITUALLY STARVING TO DEATH.

Friends Who Read Their Bibles and Pray - Another important thing to look for in people you could befriend is whether they spend personal time reading their Bible and praying. While this seems like an obvious behavior that all Christians should practice, you might be surprised at how few do it. In the next chapter, you'll discover some disturbing statistics about Christians and Bible reading. Most Christians *don't* read their Bibles every day. And many of those same Christians spend time in prayer only when they face a crisis.

Selecting friends who read their Bibles every day means having relationships with people who are grounded in their faith. They know *what* they believe, and they know *why* they believe it. Friends who read their Bibles every day can challenge you in your own personal Bible reading time; they can even answer some initial questions you have in your newfound faith. And as you'll discover in the next chapter, reading the Bible is the spiritual equivalent to your body gaining strength from eating food! It's important to have friends who are not spiritually starving to death.

Not only should you find friends who read their Bibles every day, you should find ones who pray every day. Prayer is how we talk to God. When we don't pray, we are literally giving God the silent treatment. God is the best listener, the best counselor, and the answerer of prayers. It would only make sense for you and me to share all our thoughts and emotions with the one who will listen to us without fail, give us the best advice, and give us what we need along the journey.

Since you're most likely new in your faith, you'll have questions about prayer. I'll cover prayer in greater detail later in the book. But if you want good examples of how to pray, find friends who can model that behavior for you. And since you now know that friends will either push you away from God or pull you closer to Him, don't you want ones that spend time talking with Him?

Friends Who Are Consistent - The last thing to look for in your journey towards building Jesus-centered friendships is people who are consistent in their faith. *Consistent* simply means they're the same person no matter what circumstances they face. I remember as a youth pastor having students who were the model Christian at youth group Sunday night, only to see a totally different person on social media the next week. You know the type. We call them things like posers, fakes, or hypocrites.

Some young people are merely putting on a show at church every week. Maybe they attend because their parents make them. Or they may attend because they genuinely want to grow their relationship with Jesus. Unfortunately, these types are completely different people on Monday morning or Friday night.

These are the types of people who show up to church with a smile on their face and a Bible verse in their mouth. They say and do all the right things in front of their Christian friends. They appear to worship God passionately, pray during service, and might even volunteer somewhere. They tell the pastor everything he wants to hear, and they act like they've got it all together. But two nights before church, they were getting drunk at the lake party. On Monday morning, they're telling dirty jokes and pushing unpopular kids around in the halls. Remember, Jesus said you would know people by their fruit. If someone you know shows one kind of fruit Sunday night at church but a different kind of fruit Monday morning, they're probably not the best choice to build a friendship with.

Hopefully you now have some practical things to look for in whether a person is living their faith or not. Pay attention to whether they go to church, are selective on what media they consume, whether they read their Bible and pray, and if they're consistent in their faith. If they appear to be someone who lives their faith consistently, they're a good person to partner with in your newfound faith.

SHARE THEIR FAITH

The other thing to consider and look for is if they share their faith with others. While someone living their faith is important, someone who *shares* their faith is next level. This one might be easier for you to find if the reason you got saved is someone invited you to church. If they did, they're probably a great person to build a relationship with! Look for people who bring others to church. Connect with people who post things on social media that draw people to Jesus. People who post scriptures or share content from Christian influencers might be a good place to start. Students who help at a community shelter or go on mission trips are also great examples of people who share their faith.

OFTEN PEOPLE ASK ME HOW THEY'RE SUPPOSED TO BE A LIGHT TO UNSAVED PEOPLE IF THEY ONLY HANG OUT WITH OTHER CHRISTIANS.

Making friends with people who share their faith is important because they show a spiritual maturity that goes beyond a personal relationship with Jesus. These types of people have moved into the area of making disciples (Jesus followers). People who do this are obeying Jesus' command in Matthew, "Now wherever you go, make disciples of all nations, baptizing them in the name of the Father, the Son, and the Holy Spirit."[7]

As I bring this chapter on shaking up your friendships to a close, I want to address something important. This topic often brings up questions and challenges regarding being a light and influence on those who don't follow Jesus. Often people ask me how they're supposed to be a light to unsaved people if they only hang out with other Christians. It's a great question that comes from a genuine heart.

Jesus said, "Your lives light up the world. For how can you hide a city that stands on a hilltop? And who would light a lamp and then hide it in an obscure place? Instead, it's placed where everyone in the house can benefit from its light. So don't hide your light! Let it shine brightly before others, so that your commendable works will shine as light upon them, and then they will give their praise to your Father in heaven."[8] Jesus was reminding believers that they were and

NOW WHAT?   SHAKE UP

still are supposed to share the truth with all people. The world is dark, and it needs the light and truth of the gospel of Jesus Christ.

People feel that if they only hang out with other believers, they aren't spreading their light to the darkness, and this is true. You'll reach a point in your walk with Jesus where you'll reach enough spiritual maturity to be a light to others. In fact, your recent change will be a light to some of your unsaved friends and family right away. They'll see how you've changed into a Jesus follower, and that will impact them. But, until you have reached that point of maturity, I want to encourage you to spend time with other Christians who will be a positive influence on you and who can help you grow.

In time, through the Holy Spirit's leading and advice and counsel from your pastor and parents, you can begin hanging out with people who live the opposite of your faith. Then you can shine your light in how you live and what you say. But until you've reached that point, you risk non-believers dragging you back into your old ways of living. Oftentimes we hang out with "the wrong crowd" thinking we are influencing them for Jesus, when in fact they're influencing us for the world. Don't be fooled.

Now that you have a game plan on how to shake up your
relationships for the better, let's look at your next step in this journey
of faith in Jesus. Let's talk about reading your Bible.

3

CHOW DOWN

Read your Bible.

Bread alone will not satisfy, but true life is found in every word that constantly goes forth from God's mouth.
Matthew 4:4 TPT

Back in 2009, I went on a mission trip to the country of Zambia. Zambia is in the southern region of Africa and is home to over 19 million people. Zambia is one of the top-ten countries in the world that has been impacted by the HIV/AIDS epidemic. Because of HIV/AIDS, the life expectancy rate for both men and women is only around 65 years of age. Compare that to the United States where men are expected to live to age 78, and women are expected to live to age 83. The infant mortality rate, which is the number of babies that die very soon after birth, is around five out of 1,000 in the United States. It's 38 per 1,000 in Zambia.[1,2] You can see how hopeless things are in Zambia and how important it is to share Jesus with them.

The group I traveled with (Every Orphan's Hope) hosted a Christian kids and youth camp for two weeks. The camp was very similar to a youth summer camp or vacation Bible school that American church kids might attend. We sang songs, taught messages from the Bible, did some arts and crafts, and played a lot of games.

The coolest thing that happened those two weeks was that hundreds of young people made Jesus their personal Lord and Savior, much like you recently did! We also helped a team build orphan homes in which the kids would live. Most of the kids in the village we visited lived in huts with dirt floors. The huts were smaller than most bedrooms in America. They didn't have running water or electricity. They didn't have any indoor plumbing. In fact, most of the people we met didn't have much of anything at all.

Of all the differences I saw when I was there, one struck me the hardest. Most of the kids we met were so unhealthy that we could see their rib cages. I'm sure you know what I'm talking about. You've seen the commercials on TV where some organization is trying to get you to donate money to feed starving children in Africa. The commercial shows footage of kids that look sick and have flies buzzing around them. Some of what we saw in person could have been shown on one of those commercials.

The reason those kids were so skinny is because they were malnourished and, in some cases, *literally* starving. They don't have access to the variety of foods that you do. They don't have as much food as you do, and what they do have is not as nutritious. These kids ate mostly rice and beans in smaller portions than you probably do— no second and third helpings, no extra slices of pizza. They also ate less often than you probably do.

While they *might* eat three meals a day, you and I get a couple of extra snacks in too. They have no trips to Taco Bell, no dollar menu, no chicken nuggets, and no cheeseburgers. Not to mention, there aren't a ton of ice cream and donut choices for them. And because they don't like you do in America, many of them were pretty sick.

I must say that even though the future for those kids looked hopeless, they were some of the happiest people I've ever met. Even though they didn't have any possessions like smart phones and video games, they were some of the most grateful people I've ever met. And even though they didn't have access to the food and luxuries that we do, they were some of the proudest people I've ever met.

**MANY CHRISTIANS ARE LIVING
LIFE SPIRITUALLY MALNOURISHED
AND STARVING.**

So, what does this have to do with you and the decision you have made? How does it tie into your next step in your faith? In Matthew 4, Jesus says, "It takes more than bread to stay alive. It takes a steady stream of words from God's mouth."[3] Did you catch that? Jesus said that God's words are just as important to you as eating food! And those words that God speaks are written down in the Bible. Many Christians today aren't "eating" regularly. That is, they're not feeding on God's words every day; they aren't reading their Bibles. As a result of this lack of discipline, many Christians are living life spiritually malnourished and starving.

ONLY 34 PERCENT OF GEN Z TEENS BELIEVE THAT LYING IS WRONG.

At the time this book was written, a Christian research company called Barna Group did a study that focused on Generation Z (Gen Z)—people born between the late 1990s and early 2010s. The study covered what forces influenced Gen Z as well as what made up their worldview. Barna published the results in a book titled *Gen Z – The Culture, Beliefs, and Motivations Shaping the Next Generation.* Here are some of the results:

- Out of 69 million children and teens in Gen Z, just 4 percent have a biblical worldview (i.e., believe in living the way the Bible teaches).[4]

- Only 34 percent of Gen Z teens believe that lying is wrong.[5]
- Only 16 percent of Gen Z indicates that they want to become more spiritually mature before they turn 30.[6]

You may read those statistics and not be surprised, or reading those statistics may shock you. Maybe you have no idea if those statistics are good or bad. Let me give you some other statistics of other generations from the same study, so you can compare. Here is the breakdown of what percentage of each generation has a biblical worldview:

- Baby Boomers (born 1946-1964) – 10 percent
- Generation X (vorn 1965-1980) – 7 percent
- Millennials (born 1981-1996) – 6 percent
- Generation Z (born 1997-2012) – 4 percent

Here is the breakdown of what percentage believes lying is wrong from the Silent Generation and Gen Z:

- The Silent Generation (born 1928-1945) – 61 percent
- Generation Z (born 1997-2012) – 34 percent

Here is the breakdown of what percentage wants to become more spiritually mature by age 30 from Millennials and Gen Z.

· Millennials (born 1981-1996) – 29 percent
· Generation Z (born 1997-2012) – 16 percent

The book covers far more than these three statistics, but one theme is true. Each generation in America is less "spiritual" than the one before it. Each generation in America is less familiar with the Christian faith. Each generation in America regularly attends church less frequently. And each generation in America knows less about the Bible. The reason for these results is because people are not reading their Bibles regularly.

You may still wonder *why* you need to read your Bible every day. After all, you read things in school years ago, and you still remember some of what you read. Maybe you think that you can just pick up *The Good Book* whenever you need answers or whenever you're having trouble in life. While the Bible is helpful in times of trouble, and it does provide answers to questions you might have, God gave it to you for *daily* direction.

God once told Joshua, "Study this Book of Instruction continually. Meditate on it day and night so you'll be sure to obey everything written in it. Only then will you prosper and succeed in all you do."[7] God didn't tell Joshua to read the Bible occasionally or to refer to it whenever he had a question; God told Joshua to *study* it *continually*.

EACH GENERATION IN AMERICA IS LESS "SPIRITUAL" THAN THE ONE BEFORE IT.

God said Joshua should read the Bible continually, as much as possible. God also told Joshua to meditate on what he read. *Meditation* means that God wanted Joshua to think about what he had just read. God wants the same thing for you! He wants you to read the Bible as often as you can and to spend time thinking about what you read.

God also attached a promise to reading your Bible. He said you'll succeed and prosper in all you do. How cool is that? That means that when you read your Bible and think about what you read, you'll do better in school. You'll have healthier relationships. You'll reach more of your personal goals. Your life will get better!

The Bible is God's love letter to you. In that love letter, He covers everything He wants you to know about life. It teaches you the difference between right and wrong, and it teaches you how to respond to different circumstances in life. It shows you how to overcome temptation and how to treat people. The Bible teaches you how to live and how to follow Jesus.

THE BIBLE IS YOUR INSTRUCTION MANUAL ON HOW TO LIVE.

Hopefully, you now understand why reading the Bible is important. And you now know that there are some benefits to it. But you might wonder *how* the Bible can do all these things for you. The Bible can do these things in your life by giving you direction and help. Let's see how this plays out.

DIRECTION FROM THE BIBLE

Direction comes from the Bible through what you learn. The more you learn, the more direction you'll get. It's kind of like reading the instruction manual on something. I always read the instruction manual any time I buy something like a new lawnmower or power tool. I do this because the instruction manual shows me how to put the thing together, how to operate it, and how to take care of it.

The Bible is your instruction manual on how to live. It gives you direction on how you were "put together" by God, how you operate as a person, and how you should take care of yourself. In more practical ways, the Bible will give you direction about things like what rights you have as a Jesus follower, who Jesus was and what He did, the history of the church, God's character, and more. All these things, along with teaching you how to live as a Christian, will direct you into success, just like God promised Joshua.

Paul put it this way, "All Scripture is inspired by God and is useful to teach us what is true and to make us realize what is wrong in our lives. It corrects us when we are wrong and teaches us to do what is right."[8] The Bible directs us by teaching, correcting, and helping us realize things. One example of how the Bible can provide direction in our lives is by helping us decide which path(s) to take along our journey. The Bible, along with prayer, can help us make decisions about school, work, and relationships. Believe it or not, the Bible can even help us pick the right college to attend or the right job to take or whether or not we should date someone.

Let me give you a personal example on this one. One afternoon, when I was just a couple of months away from graduating from Bible school, I received a phone call. On the other end of that call was a job opportunity at a church. I was offered a position to serve as their middle-school pastor. It was an answer to prayer, or so I thought. After all, I had quit a successful job to move to Tulsa and attend Bible school *because* I wanted to be a youth pastor. But after I got off the phone, I felt inside my heart that I wasn't supposed to accept the position at that time. I was confused, as you can imagine. I felt called to the ministry, went to school for ministry training, and had been offered my dream job. But I didn't feel like I was supposed to take it.

My parents thought I was insane for not immediately accepting the position. But each time I considered calling them back and accepting the offer, I had an unsettled feeling in my heart. I didn't have peace about it. I had a meeting with one of my instructors at Bible school, and I shared the situation with him. He counseled me a bit and then gave me a Bible verse to read. He encouraged me to read that verse and to pray about it concerning my current dilemma. So, I did exactly what he told me to do.

After my meeting with him, I quickly grabbed my Bible, opened it up to the verse, and read the following, "And let the peace (soul harmony which comes) from Christ rule (act as umpire continually) in your hearts [deciding and settling with finality all questions that arise in your minds, in that peaceful state] to which as [members of Christ's] one body you were also called [to live]."[9] As I read that verse, it hit me! I immediately got direction about my situation. I knew that I didn't have peace about accepting the position, and I realized that I shouldn't make any big decisions in life *without* peace. I went to the Bible about my situation, and when I did, God's Word gave me direction and help.

Reading that verse showed me that it's almost as if Jesus' spirit living in our hearts is like an umpire at a baseball game. Instead of calling balls and strikes, He "calls" through peace what is the right or wrong decision to make. He does this by either giving us peace or not giving us peace. After reading that verse and praying about it, I knew that I wasn't supposed to accept that position.

This is just one example of how the Bible gives you direction. It will direct you down the best path for your life. It will direct you by showing you how to pray about things. It will direct you by reminding you of what Jesus did for you at the cross. It will direct you by encouraging you to show fruits of the Spirit, like joy and peace, in the middle of a rough life event. Not only will the Bible give you direction, but it will also give you help.

READING THAT VERSE SHOWED ME THAT IT'S ALMOST AS IF JESUS' SPIRIT LIVING IN OUR HEARTS IS LIKE AN UMPIRE AT A BASEBALL GAME.

HELP FROM THE BIBLE

I've now given you a few examples on how the Bible provides direction. Now let's look at how it helps you. The two major ways it helps you is by *lighting up things* and *sifting things*. The Bible is unlike *any* other book that has ever been written. Some books are filled with information, while other books are filled with motivation. Textbooks are a great example of books that have tons of information like dates and facts.

Books that are considered self-help books are filled with motivation. Books that teach you how to manage your time or how to lose weight fall under this category. The Bible is full of both *information* and *motivation*, but it was written through *inspiration*. This means that the men who wrote the books of the Bible were *inspired* by God to write them. God literally spoke to the authors and told them what to write down. Isn't that amazing? The Bible is the only book that can make this claim.

Because the Bible is *inspired*, it's known as a living book. This just means that it never goes out of style or becomes irrelevant. Like I said in the first chapter, the Bible covers *every* topic of life you can think of! The Bible *never* goes out of style. The Bible is full of truths that have *never* been proven false and never will!

Did you know that the Bible talked about the earth being round *long* before people sailed the world to prove it wasn't flat? The prophet Isaiah wrote, "God sits above the *circle* of the earth"[10] (emphasis added). That's just one example. The Bible is a living book because God wrote it, it never goes out of style, and it's full of truth. It's also a living book because it's the only book in the world that delivers on its promises. The Bible is the only book that will give you exactly what it says it will give you if you do exactly what it says you should do. No other book can make that claim.

Since the Bible is inspired by God and considered a living book, it will do things to you when you read it. It will do things that no other book can do. It will help you be the best Jesus follower you can be. When you read the Bible, it will change your mind and feed your spirit.

The Bible will change your mind by brainwashing you. You read that right! Just like how any *information* you take in can change how you think, the information you get from the Bible will change your mind. The book of Romans encourages you not to think like the rest of the world does but to *renew your mind,* "Don't copy the behavior and customs of this world, but let God transform you into a new person by changing the way you think."[11]

Renewing your mind is simply changing your mind. For example, you might have always believed that if someone does something bad to you, you should get even with them. But the Bible says, "Love your enemy, bless the one who curses you, do something wonderful for the one who hates you."[12] You'll change your mind

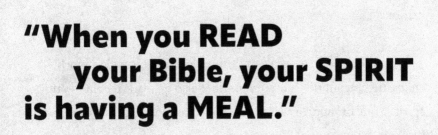

"When you READ your Bible, your SPIRIT is having a MEAL."

about how to treat your enemies just by reading that one verse.

Whenever you read a book, your soul is at work. It's your soul that captures the information you read. Your brain processes facts while your emotions respond to emotional material. If you read a suspense novel, your soul can get anxious. If you read a love story, your soul can get happy or sad. If you read a textbook in science class, your brain processes and stores information that hopefully you can recall later.

Whenever you read the Bible, your soul is still at work changing your mind, but your spirit is also at work feeding your spirit. Your brain processes facts like dates and names; your emotions respond to emotional material, such as when Jesus heals someone; and your spirit receives something too. Your spirit is nourished, informed, strengthened, inspired, and more! Remember, the Bible is food—we read that in Matthew 4:4.

When you read your Bible, your spirit is having a meal. That's why people who read their Bibles are better able to overcome temptation and sin. That's why people who read their Bibles "feel" closer to God. That's why people who read their Bibles tend to be more engaged in their faith. Their spirits are getting fed and are growing stronger! Remember that the health and maturity of your spirit is directly tied to how much time you spend reading and studying your Bible.

THE THING ABOUT PATHS IS THAT IF YOU STAY ON THEM, YOU'LL REACH YOUR DESTINATION.

Lighting Up Things - I said earlier that the Bible provides direction and helps you in practical ways. I talked about how it shows you what paths to take in life. I even gave you an example of how I used the Bible to help me decide about taking a job offer. Whenever I talk about paths in life, I literally picture a path somewhere out in the woods. Do you? Can you picture a path right now? I see a dirt path moving through a wooded area, much like the ones I had in my backyard when I was a kid.

The thing about paths is that if you stay on them, you'll reach your destination. But, if you get off the path, you can get lost. You'll have to spend time finding your way back to the path before you can get to your destination. Getting off track leads to fear, frustration, and fatigue. Life has many paths, and God wants you to pick the *best* one. Just like I used the Bible to choose the right career path, you can use it for the different paths in your life.

The Bible is designed to give you direction to choose the right path and help to keep you on that path no matter what happens. If you're walking on a path in the woods, you might come across a fallen tree. That tree now stands in your way. You might also face some bad weather along your path. There could be fog that limits what you can see ahead of you, or there might be heavy rain that makes the path hard to walk on.

The time of day you walk your path makes a difference too. If you start walking on your path in the evening, you risk it getting too dark to see before you reach your destination. Real paths in life, like the wooded path analogy, can include obstacles and difficulties along the way to your destination. Using what you read in the Bible can help you stay on your path or get back on track if needed.

For example, the Bible can shine some light if things get

"foggy" or "dark." The Psalmist once wrote, "Your word is a lamp to guide my feet and a light for my path."[13] The Bible shines light on whatever path you are on, showing you the dangers and illuminating the right way to go. The Bible will light the way you are headed in life to show you things you wouldn't otherwise see. Just like you might not see that fallen tree on your path in the dark woods, you might not see an unhealthy relationship in life that's trying to trip you up. When you read and study your Bible, it will "shine a light" in the dark places along your path to help keep you from tripping up or getting off track.

USING WHAT YOU READ IN THE BIBLE CAN HELP YOU STAY ON YOUR PATH OR GET YOU BACK ON TRACK IF NEEDED.

Sifting Things - The other way the Bible provides help along your path is by sifting things for you. Sticking with our wooded path analogy, what if you were walking down the path because someone told you it was the best way to get to your destination? You've probably been in a situation like this before. You knew where you wanted to go, so you asked someone for directions.

The person told you which route to take, but Google Maps recommended a different route. Now, the whole time you are walking the path the person recommended, you're wondering if you're taking the best route. You start second guessing if you should have gone the other way. You question which advice you should have taken; you might even get confused on the source of both routes. Did Google Maps tell me to go this way, or was it the person I asked for directions?

You can run into the same scenario in life. You might have the urge to apply to a particular college, or maybe you feel like you should go to Bible school. Maybe you have a desire to be a youth pastor, or you feel a strong pull to become a doctor. Your friends give you advice, your parents give you advice, and you have your own plans in your mind. After a while, you question if God is telling you to do something or if it's your own desire.

Have you ever thought or wondered about something and even questioned if that thought was a good one or a bad one? You thought to yourself, "Is the devil tempting me? Is this something that

I want to do or that he wants me to do?" Times like these can be very confusing. This is one of the most common questions I get from students. They want to know how to know the difference between what God is telling them, what the devil is telling them, and what they are telling themselves.

The Bible will provide help with these situations by sifting things for you. It will tell you who is "talking" in these moments. The book of Hebrews puts it this way: "For the word of God is alive and powerful. It is sharper than the sharpest two-edged sword, cutting between soul and spirit, between joint and marrow. It exposes our innermost thoughts and desires."[14] To get a better idea of sifting, picture one of my favorite candies—Skittles.

I *love* Skittles, but my favorite flavor is red. When I open a bag of Skittles, one of the first things I do is separate all the colors. I like to set aside all the red Skittles so that I can eat them last. The process of separating all the colors is the same idea as sifting something. When you read the Bible, it takes your spirit, soul, and body, and then it separates them like Skittles. The Bible helps you see which desires come from your spirit, which desires come from your soul, and which desires come from your body.

That verse says the Bible cuts or divides between soul and spirit. For example, let's say somebody says something untrue about you. They gossip about you all over school, resulting in people believing the lie. It can be frustrating when you character is being attacked by someone. The fact that a lie is being spread about you can cause some strong emotions. You could experience anything from embarrassment to anger.

Now, let's say you feel like the way you should retaliate is to spread untruths about that person. Would God tell you to gossip about that person in return? Would your born-again spirit tell you to do that? Or is it more likely that either the devil or your own emotions are getting the better of you?

If you take the situation I just described and go to the Bible to see what it says, you'll get both direction and help. If you google "What does the Bible say about . . ." and look up gossip or retaliation, you'll probably find several verses about your circumstance. For example, the Bible says, "Don't repay evil for evil. Don't retaliate with insults when people insult you. Instead, pay them back with a blessing. That is what God has called you to do, and he will grant you his blessing."[15] Now you know that it wouldn't be right to retaliate by gossiping about the person who gossiped about you.

Another place your search might lead you is the book of Proverbs where it says, "Fire goes out without wood, and quarrels disappear when gossip stops."[16] Now you have two places in the Bible that direct you to not gossip about the person who spread lies about you. But what about the feelings you're dealing with? What about the anger you have towards the person who lied about you? Is that your spirit, or is that your soul?

The Bible says that the fruit of the Holy Spirit displays through our spirit, certain characteristics. "But the Holy Spirit produces this kind of fruit in our lives: love, joy, peace, patience, kindness, goodness, faithfulness, gentleness, and self-control. There is no law against these things!"[17] Obviously, *anger* is not listed, so the Bible is helping you decide where this emotional response is coming from and helping you divide between if it's coming from your soul or your spirit.

The book of Galatians also says, "When you follow the desires of your sinful nature, the results are very clear: sexual immorality, impurity, lustful pleasures, idolatry, sorcery, hostility, quarreling, jealousy, outbursts of anger, selfish ambition, dissension, division, envy, drunkenness, wild parties, and other sins like these."[18] In other words, anger comes from your soul or your emotions. Another way it's said is that anger comes from your flesh (your own desires).

As you see, we can take one bad situation that could happen in your life, observe how you want to respond to it, then check the Bible to see what it has to say about how to respond. In this way, the Bible is providing direction and help.

SOME PRACTICAL STEPS

Now that you know how important reading your Bible is and understand how it can work in your life by directing and helping you, let me close this chapter with some practical tips to get you started. First, you should know that the Bible is not to be read like any other book. There are many Bible-reading plans that have you start in Genesis and end in Revelation. I don't suggest starting with one of those plans.

The first practical step is deciding what order to read the books of the Bible. Since you're new in your faith in Jesus, I encourage you to start reading in the Gospels. This means you should start reading in Matthew and then read through to the end of John. The reason I suggest this is because the Gospels (Matthew, Mark, Luke, and John) are all about the life and works of Jesus.

FIRST, YOU SHOULD KNOW THAT THE BIBLE IS NOT TO BE READ LIKE ANY OTHER BOOK.

The life of a Christian is all about being a Jesus follower; that's what the word *Christian* means. If you're going to be successful at following Jesus, you need to know as much about Him as you can. The best way to build a relationship with someone is to spend time with them. Daily times of prayer and reading about Jesus are how you spend time with Him.

Keep in mind that you can and should repeat the Gospels as many times as you like. This helps you pick up something new each time. You'll re-read parts of the Bible for the rest of your life, so get used to repeating what you have already read. The goal of Bible reading is not to read the whole thing as quickly as you can. The goal is to spend time in God's Word so that it can bring change to your life and personality.

Once you feel like you have spent a good amount of time in the Gospels, move on to the Epistles. *Epistle* means letter, and much of the New Testament is letters from specific authors to churches. The Epistles were written by people like the Apostle Paul, Peter the disciple, and others. They were written as God inspired them to write, and they were written to churches during the day these men lived. Since they're letters to churches, they're full of ideas on how to be a Jesus follower. And since you're new in your faith, these ideas will be a big help.

The next practical step is figuring out which version of the Bible is best for you to read. There are literally dozens of versions of the Bible. One of the most well-known versions, the King James Version, is probably what you're familiar with. It's the most quoted version around. The King James Version is where many of the *thou*s and *hitherto*s come from. As you can imagine, I do not recommend that version if you're new to your faith.

For someone in your position, I recommend either the New Living Translation or The Passion Translation. There are two reasons for this. First, these are *translations*, not paraphrases. A translation is where a group of people take the original languages the Bible was written in and re-word it into the way we talk today. Even though they re-word it, the meanings and definitions are the same as the original. This way what we read in the Bible today means the same thing it meant when it was written. It would be like taking the vocabulary words of a Spanish science textbook and translating those words into English.

THE GOAL IS TO SPEND TIME IN GOD'S WORD SO THAT IT CAN BRING CHANGE TO YOUR LIFE AND PERSONALITY.

A paraphrase works a little differently. It still begins with the original languages the Bible was written in, but it rewords them into the way we talk today, and it *changes* the "vocabulary words" to sound more modern and even trendy. It's like taking a vocabulary word from the science textbook that's written in Spanish and changing it to a different word, *and then* translating that new word into English. While Bible paraphrases sometimes sound cooler and more poetic, they might not use the same words that were originally written.

I ENCOURAGE YOU TO FIND WHAT TIME OF THE DAY WORKS BEST FOR YOU TO READ YOUR BIBLE.

Second, the two translations I recommend are in modern English, so they're easier to understand than other translations. There is no one version of the Bible that is the absolute best over the others. In fact, as you grow and mature in your faith, you'll find yourself using different versions on occasion. This is a great way to study Bible verses by seeing how each version teaches the same idea. Eventually you'll find which version *you* like best; in the meantime, try the New Living Translation or The Passion Translation. I believe they will help you succeed in putting your daily Bible reading into practice.

This brings us to our last practical step of Bible reading and helps us close this chapter. I encourage you to find what time of the day works best for you to read your Bible. Then, schedule that time every day. Some people's brains are more awake and creative in the morning. Some people do better at night. Find what works for you, and stick with it.

Young people tend to stay up later than the rest of the family, so that may work for you. Or maybe you like to wake up earlier than your siblings to get first dibs at the shower. Whatever time of day you choose, schedule out 10-15 minutes to read your Bible. Start in the Gospels, with a version you enjoy reading, and get at it! You'll see your mind start changing, your spirit start growing, and your paths start lighting up.

Now that you have your Bible reading down, let's talk about the TenByTen Challenge.

4

TENBYTEN

Pray and worship.

But Jesus often slipped away from them and went into the wilderness to pray.
Luke 5:16 TPT

When I was in Bible school, I had a teacher who changed my thinking about how I spent my time. One day during class, he challenged us all to spend more time in prayer and Bible reading. During his challenge, you could sense the resistance in the room. You could even hear a group of grumbles sweep through the class. My teacher decided to take the opportunity to show the class just how much time we had in a week, and how much time we wasted within that week. He started off by writing down exactly how many hours there are in a week, and I'd like to do that with you now. Now hang tight because we're going to do some math.

There are 24 hours in a day and 7 days in a week. So, there are 168 hours in a week.

He reminded us that every single person in the world gets 168 hours. No one gets more; no one gets less. It's just a matter of *how* each person uses those 168 hours. He then took the most common life needs and tasks the average person has, and he began breaking them down by how many hours a day or week they take. For example:

- The average person sleeps 8 hours a day.
- The average person either works or goes to school 8 hours a day.
- The average person spends 3 hours a day eating.
- The average person spends 1 hour a day in the bathroom.

At this point, I hope you get the point. No two people spend the exact same amount of time on each category as the next person. We are all unique and have different schedules. For example, you might spend more than eight hours a day sleeping. Or an adult might not have homework after school, but a student in school doesn't have to spend time cooking dinner for the family.

IT'S JUST A MATTER OF HOW EACH PERSON USES THOSE 168 HOURS.

What my teacher challenged us to do was to add up our own personal schedules to see how we spent our week. We then took the total amount of hours we spent on our unique tasks and subtracted them from the total 168 hours in a week. At the time I did this exercise in class, I found that I had at least 10 hours left in my week.

TIME EXERCISE

So, before I talk about the TenByTen Challenge, I want you to do this exercise on your own. Use the page I have provided called "Time Exercise." Begin by writing down all your categories in the

TIME EXERCISE

Category	Duration
_____	_____
_____	_____
_____	_____
_____	_____
_____	_____
_____	_____
_____	_____
_____	_____
_____	_____
_____	_____

first column. List whatever you can think of. Here are some examples of what you might include:

- Sleeping
- School/Work
- Eating
- Bathroom
- Homework
- Chores
- Social Media
- TV
- Family Time

Then, next to the column of tasks you have, write down the amount of time it takes EACH DAY to perform these tasks. Once you have all the tasks you can think of, add up the total amount of hours. If your total amount is greater than 24, you'll have to adjust since there are only 24 hours in a day. Once you've reached a total that is less than 24, write it down. Go ahead and put this book down, and work out your figures.

Now that you're back, consider what the number you came

up with represents. That number represents your free time. It's the extra time you have left in the day to do with however want! You could use that time to take up a hobby. You could use it to get some extra sleep. You could use it to hang out with your friends. Or you could use it to spend time growing in your new faith.

This chapter is all about what I call the TenByTen Challenge. It's where I challenge students to take ten minutes every day to pray and ten minutes to worship. The reason that I had you flesh out what your average day looks like is because I want to stop your first excuse dead in its tracks. The excuse I am often given when I throw out this challenge is that they don't have enough time, or they say that they are too busy.

What most of you probably found out after doing the exercise is that you have more time left in the day than you realized. Even if your task list added up to 24 hours and you're reading this thinking you *literally* don't have enough time in the day for praying and worshipping God, you can review your list and see where you can trim things a bit.

Maybe you listed two hours of social media a day. Cut 30

minutes out of that to give to prayer and worship. Maybe you take an hour-long shower. Turn that into a 30-minute shower, and you're good to go. The point is that you either already have enough time to give to TenByTen or you can *make* that time.

THERE IS NOTHING LIKE BEING ABLE TO POUR YOUR HEART OUT TO THE BEST LISTENER IN THE UNIVERSE.

Now that we have your main excuse out of the way, let's talk about what TenByTen is. TenByTen is where you set aside ten minutes for praying and ten minutes for worship. This step is all about encouraging you to spend time with the one who changed your life. This step is where you get to spend time every day talking to God in prayer. It's where you also get to spend time every day thanking God through worship.

This chapter began with a Bible verse that reminds us that Jesus often got away from everyone and everything to go spend time in prayer and worship. If Jesus made the time to do these things, it's important that we do too. I encourage you to set aside this time each day to get into a private setting and put prayer and worship to practice. I'll be honest with you; this will be tough at first. You'll find every reason to put it off or avoid it. And once you do get started, you might be bored at first. But keep at it! It will get easier and more enjoyable the more you do it.

PRACTICAL TIPS

Let me share some practical tips to help you get going. First, try and set a timer. Most people find it difficult to pray for as long as ten minutes when they first get started. You might find that you don't know what to pray about or you run out of things to cover. You may find that you feel like you don't know *how* to pray. What ends up happening is that you talk to God about whatever you can think of and then call it good. The problem is that it might only take you a couple of minutes.

Timing - If you set a timer when you first start doing the TenByTen, it will challenge you to keep going until you hit the ten-minute mark. And with time and practice, you'll find that you'll eventually start praying beyond your ten minutes. Everybody finds that when praying, one of the best places to be is somewhere private.

There is nothing like being able to pour your heart out to the best listener in the universe. There is nothing like the peace you experience when you give God your worries. And there is no greater joy in life than to see your prayers answered! When you get results in prayer, you'll want to keep coming back.

The next practical thing I encourage you to do is make a list of what you want to pray and talk to God about. There is nothing wrong with writing things down. God doesn't mind at all! Writing things down will help you keep from forgetting them when you finally get to pray about them. List all the names of the people you want to pray for. List the things you want to ask God for help. List the concerns and worries you want to share with Him. When you get to your time and place for prayer, pull out your list, and go through it one by one.

Wording - Another great tip for prayer is to use Bible verses in your prayers to God. Jesus did this when He prayed, and you can too. Take any Bible verse that covers the topic you want to talk to God about, and use it in your prayer with Him. For example, maybe you're anxious about an upcoming science exam. In your Bible reading time, you come across Philippians 4:13 which says, "For I can do everything through Christ, who gives me strength." Write that Bible verse down, and bring it with you into your prayer time.

There are a couple of reasons you'll want to use Bible verses in your prayers. The first reason is that it reminds you of something God has promised. Faith is believing God will do what He said He will do. When you know *what* God promises about something, it strengthens your faith. Another way to look at it is that knowing what the Bible says about something is the same as knowing what God personally promises you.

Have your parents ever made a promise to you? Do they usually deliver on their promises? Do you ever worry that they won't? Usually, if your parents make you a promise, you *expect* the thing they promise. That's because parents hardly lie to you. It's like when you were a kid at Christmastime. You knew that you would find Christmas presents under the tree on Christmas morning because your parents told you that you were getting presents.

You didn't worry that there wouldn't be any presents to open because your parents wouldn't lie to you. You *expected* to see things under the tree when you woke up. But your parents are human and not perfect. So even though they probably wouldn't lie to you on purpose, they can make mistakes. Some things are out of their control, and sometimes they *can't* deliver on their promises.

FAITH IS BELIEVING GOD WILL DO WHAT HE SAID HE WILL DO.

God is *not* a human and *is* perfect! While your parents can fail to deliver on a promise, God *never* fails. And if you still trust your parents when they make a promise, think about how much you should trust God! I didn't make up any of this about God. The Bible says, "God is not a man, so he does not lie. He is not human, so he does not change his mind. Has he ever spoken and failed to act? Has he ever promised and not carried it through?"[1] That's *great* news!

Include Bible verses in your prayers to strengthen your faith, and remind yourself what God promised you. If you're anxious about your upcoming science exam, read Philippians 4:13 and realize that you can pass it because Jesus will help you! Now you can pray that Bible verse in your prayer time and strengthen your faith in God's faithful promises.

The other reason you'll want to use Bible verses in your prayers is because God's words are more powerful than your own. Do you have a little brother or sister? Are they smaller than you? Are they weaker than you? Have they ever tried to tell you to do something? It usually doesn't go over very well, does it?

Mia and I have three girls. They are all under the age of six at the time of writing this book. Occasionally our two-year old will try to tell our five-year old what to do. It makes us all laugh out loud because our two-year old has no power over our five-year old. She can't really *make* her older sister do anything. She's not strong enough and can't enforce her commands on her older sister.

The same thing is true with us. If we are concerned about a situation and want to change it with *our* words, we won't have much of an impact. That's because there is no power or authority behind our own words. But when we use God's words, things must change! He is the King of the universe. Whatever He says goes.

Isaiah once wrote, "The rain and snow come down from the heavens and stay on the ground to water the earth. They cause the grain to grow, producing seed for the farmer and bread for the hungry. IT IS THE SAME WITH MY WORD. I send it out, and it always produces fruit. It will accomplish all I want it to, and it will prosper everywhere I send it"[2] (emphasis added).

There is power behind your prayers, and there is power behind God's own words. Remember, the real you is a spirit that can't be seen with your eyes. There is also a whole spiritual world that can't be seen with your eyes. All kinds of things happen in that unseen world every day! Things change in that unseen world when you pray; and when you use God's words, you can change them in ways you need.

Scheduling - Another tip for praying is to find the best time in the day that works for you. If you're a morning person, then you might want to pray first thing in the morning. If you have trouble waking up in the morning, or if the house is too busy with everyone getting ready for school, you might consider praying at night before you go to bed. Maybe it's hard to find privacy because you have siblings you share spaces with. Then maybe praying in the shower is the right fit for you. Or, if you have your license, you might be able to pray in the car on your way to school.

You need to find both the time of day that works the best for you and the best place for you to pray. The Bible says, "But Jesus often withdrew to lonely places and prayed."[3] In other words, He got away from all the people so that He could have privacy with God. If you have woods in your backyard, great! If not, you might have to find a different place. Get creative and find what works best for you.

THERE IS POWER BEHIND YOUR PRAYERS, AND THERE IS POWER BEHIND GOD'S OWN WORDS.

The last practical tip deals with *how* to pray. At this point, you have your lists and Bible verses, you've picked the time of day, and, hopefully, you have your private location. Now *what?* Now you must open your mouth and start talking to God. But what does that look and sound like? It's easier than you think, and it's easier than most people make it.

While God is *the* God of the entire universe, He is also your dad. The Bible calls Him our Heavenly Father. Since prayer is simply talking to God, talk to Him like you would your own dad, a family member, or a friend. You don't have to act all religious and use big theological words. You can just talk to Him like you would if you were having a video chat with a friend. And just like how you'll get better at praying for more than ten minutes, you'll also get better at praying in general. It will become more natural to you.

PRAYER EXAMPLE

Here is a short example of how you might pray about that science exam I mentioned:

Father God,

Hi! It's me. I just wanted to spend some time with You to talk about my day. I've had some ups and downs, but overall it's been good. Thanks for being with me all day and helping me out with the things I couldn't do on my own. I'm a little nervous about this upcoming science exam. As You know, it's not my favorite subject. I have paid attention in class and have taken good notes. I've been quizzing myself on the vocabulary words, and I am pretty sure I know how I'll answer the essay questions. But

I'm still nervous.

I know Your Word says that I can do all things through Jesus who gives me strength. So, I'm asking for some strength to study and to take the exam. I know You're good and faithful and love me, and I believe that You'll help me like You said You would. I can do it!

Thanks for listening to me and hearing me. I love You.

In Jesus' name, amen.

Do you see how easy it can be? It doesn't have to be complicated. If you're making the time to pray, and you genuinely want to spend time with God, He will help you along the way. It's amazing to think, He even helps us pray!

REASONS FOR PRAYER

I've talked about the TenByTen Challenge and given you some practical tips on how to get started in prayer. But before we move on to the worship portion, I want to emphasize some reasons *why* we pray. They're simple, and they can all be found in the Bible.

The most obvious reason we pray is because God has told us
to in the Bible. In a way, praying is a commandment. The apostle Paul
wrote, "Don't worry about anything; instead, pray about everything.
Tell God what you need and thank him for all he has done."[4] God
made it very clear to us in the Bible that Christians shouldn't worry
about things in life. Instead, Christians are told to pray.

Another reason we pray is to ask God for what we need. God
is our Provider, and He set up the system of how we receive things
from Him—by asking Him. It's a lot like your relationship with your
parents. You can't take the car out on Friday night unless you ask!

Jesus put it this way: "Yes, ask me for anything in my name,
and I will do it!"[5] There will be times in your life where God will bless
you even though you didn't ask. But most of the time, you need to
ask Him in prayer for what it is you need in life. Why? Because that's
how God set it up! "Yet you don't have what you want because you
don't ask God for it."[6]

The final reason we pray is because it's how we talk with
God. I remember having a conversation with a student one night
after youth group. We were catching up on some family issues he was

having when I mentioned a friend of his. He gave me a strange look and said, "We're not really friends anymore." I asked him why, and he responded by saying, "We haven't spoken in months."

Isn't it funny how quickly you can grow apart from someone? One day you're best friends, and the next day you're not. Sometimes this happens because you have a falling out. Maybe they betray you or do something to hurt you. But other times we grow apart from someone because we stop talking to them. It's hard to consider someone a friend who never talks to you or spends time with you. It's no different with God.

If you want to keep your relationship going and growing with God, you need to spend time with Him. One of the best ways to spend time with Him is to talk to Him. And one of the best ways to talk to Him is through prayer. Another way you can talk to God is through worship, and that's what we'll wrap up this chapter with.

WORSHIP

The first part of your TenByTen Challenge is to spend ten minutes a day in prayer. The second part of that challenge is to spend ten minutes a day in worship. I understand that since you're reading this book, you're probably new in your faith. So, if you don't mind, I'd like to take a little time to define worship. We touched on it in the first chapter, but let's dig a little deeper.

A famous Anglican bishop by the name of William Temple once wrote, "To worship is to quicken the conscience by the holiness of God, to feed the mind with the truth of God, to purge the imagination by the beauty of God, to open the heart to the love of God, to devote the will to the purpose of God."[7]

IT'S HARD TO CONSIDER SOMEONE A FRIEND WHO NEVER TALKS TO YOU OR SPENDS TIME WITH YOU.

That's a deep quote, and you may need to read it a few times to appreciate what Temple is saying. Among the things he is trying to explain is that worship is the act of a person focusing on God. And during that focus, the person shows appreciation to God for who He is and what He has done.

Worship has several definitions. The whole life of a Christian can be considered worship. A person volunteering or donating money to a church can be considered an act of worship. And the act of a group of people singing a worship song together in church is considered worship. There is also a private practice of singing worship songs to God, and that is the subject of the TenByTen Challenge.

I encourage you to spend ten minutes each day worshipping God. This is a time where you literally sing to God, either on your own or along with a worship song or playlist. You don't have to be a good singer to worship God. If that were true, I would be disqualified. All you must have is a desire to focus on God and a heart of gratitude towards Him. And after the life change you recently experienced, this should be an easy task.

Much like your ten minutes in prayer, I encourage you to find the best time of day and a nice private place to worship. Again, this can be in the shower or in your car or in your bedroom. Whatever works for you! Worship can be as simple as saying *thank you* to God repeatedly. Or, more realistically, you can turn on your worship playlist and sing along to the songs. Playing worship music helps you

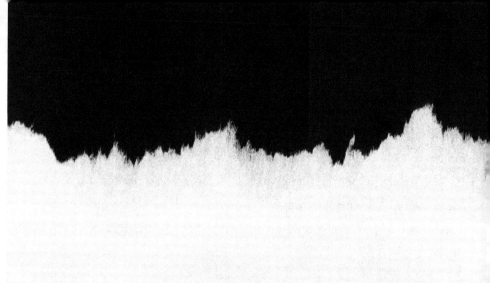

"You DON'T have to be
a GOOD singer
to WORSHIP God."

get your focus off the concerns of your busy life and onto God. Playing worship music also helps to drown out your own voice if you happen to sing like me!

Aside from finding the best time and place to worship, the most practical tip I can give you is to build a worship playlist that you enjoy and that helps you get into your "groove." While I can't personally endorse any artist or album, I have provided in the appendix, a list of popular (at the time of writing this book) worship artists for you to research.

We worship because He is worthy. God is holy, good, and loving, and He deserves our worship. He deserves more worship than we can give Him. We also worship because we love Him. He is our Heavenly Father, and He is good to us. Worship is a great way to show Him our love and attention. And we worship because the Bible tells us to: "You must worship the Lord your God and serve only him."[8] Make no mistake; worship is more of a reminder for us than it is anything God *needs*. God is the Creator of the universe, so there is nothing that we can give Him that He doesn't already have.

One of the amazing things about God is that while worship is supposed to be all about Him, He still takes the opportunity to bless you. You'll find that when you spend private time worshipping God, He'll return things to you like peace, rest, and confidence. Consider one of the things you enjoy doing the most, something that recharges you. Now multiply that experience, and you'll begin to understand how you can feel when you spend time face-to-face with God.

I encourage you to get started on your TenByTen right away. Don't put it off any longer. Find your time of day and private place to spend time in prayer and worship. Get your prayer list written out, and include your Bible verses. Get your worship playlist made, and get started. This is an important step in your newfound faith, and it will help you grow and mature, and it will set you in the right direction. Remember, the fruit of your life is directly tied to the time you spend with God.

Speaking of direction, let's look at what it means to head in the right direction in the next chapter.

5

180°

Repent
(Change your ways).

And now you must repent and turn back to God so that your sins will be removed, and so that times of refreshing will stream from the Lord's presence.
Acts 3:19 TPT

My dad loved taking me fishing when I was a kid. Some of my more memorable fishing trips happened on Lake Michigan. If you're not familiar with the Great Lakes around Michigan, you must check them out! People unfamiliar with them are often shocked when they see them in person for the first time. Don't picture the little lake you like water tubing on in the summer. Picture a small ocean that doesn't have any salt. That's how big the Great Lakes are!

Fishing trips to Lake Michigan as a kid were always an adventure. First, I had to wake up very early in the morning, usually around four in the morning! Then we'd drive to one of the cities on the coast, about an hour away from where I lived. We'd launch the boat into a channel and take the boat out into the open waters. These fishing trips were always full of action. The waves were often choppy enough to bring water over the side of our little bass boat. I am known to have lost a fishing pole or two, and I hate to admit this to you, but those waves often made me seasick. One year my dad gave me some motion-sickness medicine, and I ended up sleeping in the boat the whole trip.

Another piece of adventure these trips provided was the fog. Man, I remember a lot of fog on Lake Michigan as a kid. Sometimes the fog was as thick as a blanket. You couldn't see ten feet in front of you. If you weren't careful, you could get your positioning mixed up in the blanket of fog that surrounded you. Today, that might not be a problem, but when I was a kid, there was no such thing as Google

Maps. We didn't have smart phones or even cell phones back then.

Since Lake Michigan is so big, you can't see across the lake to the other side. If you look out of the boat away from the Michigan coastline, all you can see is water and the horizon, much like the ocean. Add fog to the mix, and you can easily get confused which way north, south, east, and west are.

On one fishing trip I remember vividly, Dad asked me to steer the boat while he and his friend set up the fishing poles. Dad gave me just one rule, "Matthew, keep your eye on the compass." He then gave me the coordinate on the compass to follow, and he told me to steer the boat either left or right in order to keep it on that point on the compass. That way the boat would keep going straight, and then the fishing lines wouldn't get tangled up. That's the great thing about a compass; it helps you stay on the right path and head in the right direction when you can't see in front of you.

Since there was so much fog that morning, I couldn't pick a spot on the horizon to shoot for. Everything was either water or gray sky, so Dad made sure I had something to go by—the coordinate on the compass. There was one problem though. I was a young boy on an adventure. Young boys (or girls) on adventures tend to let their imaginations wander. And when your imagination wanders, you don't pay attention to what's most important.

I can't tell you what I was thinking about or what I was doing that morning. What I can tell you is that I wasn't paying attention to the coordinates on the compass. After ten or fifteen minutes of just holding the steering wheel and letting the waves toss the boat wherever they wanted, I started hearing some choice words coming from my dad. He started using what I like to call "sentence enhancers."

REPENTING MEANS TURNING AWAY FROM SOMETHING.

"Matthew! What are you doing?" he cried. I turned around to find Dad and his friend *literally* tangled up in fishing line. Apparently, I had been steering the boat in a *literal* circle the whole time.

We have many routes we can take in life. Remember how we talked about the different paths in Chapter Three? We can head in the right direction, or we can head in the wrong direction. Making Jesus the Lord of your life is the first of many steps you'll take in heading in the right direction. But it's important to know that it's not the *only* step you need to take. Throughout your whole life, you're going to take steps that get you off track and headed in the wrong direction, and you're going to take steps that get you back on track and headed in the right direction. Much like the need for using a compass on a boat while in the fog, you'll need to use the tools you're learning in this book to chart your course.

Those tools include attending church, reading your Bible, and praying. Another important tool, and your next step in this book, is the act of doing a 180° turn. You have probably heard the term one-eighty before. It's the idea of turning completely around, in the opposite direction of where you were going. The Bible uses the words *repent* or *repentance* to land the same point. Repeatedly, it talks about how Jesus teaches people to "repent of their sins." But what exactly does that mean?

Repenting means turning away from something. The original

word that Jesus used for repenting means to "reconsider, to think differently afterwards."[1] In other words, now that you're a Christian, you need to think differently about some things. You need to think differently about what you watch and read. You need to think differently about how you talk and what you talk about. To put it another way, you need to do what it says in 1 Peter 1:14, "So you must live as God's obedient children. Don't slip back into your old ways of living to satisfy your own desires. You didn't know any better then."

If you were telling dirty jokes before you became a Christian, it's time to turn away from that now that you're a Jesus follower. If you were being selfish with your time and with the things you own, it's time to turn away from that and become a more giving person. One way the Bible puts it is, "Run from anything that stimulates youthful lusts."[2] If something tempts you to do something stupid or that goes against your faith, *run* from it!

Repenting is like changing course on a road trip. If we were to start in Chicago and drive towards Detroit, we would need to drive east. If we started our trip heading west, we'd have a problem. We wouldn't be heading *towards* Detroit; we'd be heading *away* from it.

"It's **NOT** about
the **OUTCOME** as much as
it is about your **HEART**."

We'd need to do a 180° turn or repent to head in the right direction.

For example, let's say you struggle with gossip. Repenting from gossip means turning away from it. Avoid it. Stop it. Quit it. Don't participate in it. Or as it says in 1 Peter 2:1, "So get rid of all evil behavior. Be done with all deceit, hypocrisy, jealousy, and all unkind speech." That's repenting. If you have been looking at pornography, you need to repent. That doesn't mean you only do it occasionally. It means you stop doing it completely. No more.

Repenting doesn't mean that you must be a perfect, sinless person. There is only one sinless person, and His name is Jesus. It's important to know that even as a Christian, you're still going to make mistakes and bad choices. It's not about the outcome as much as it is about your heart. This is where grace comes in.

GRACE FOR THE 180°

As a new Christian you'll learn to maintain an important balance in your life. That balance is to try to live as holy and as pure of a life as you can without being too hard on yourself *when* you fail. It's a difficult balance to maintain because nobody is perfect. You can't be holy and pure on your own. That's why Jesus did what He did on the cross.

That's why you decided to make Him Lord and Savior of your life. You're holy and pure *through* what He did for you. He is your substitute. You'll mess up, but God doesn't want you to give up because you messed up. Giving up on trying to live the right way will result in living your old way of life again.

REPENTING DOESN'T MEAN THAT YOU MUST BE A PERFECT, SINLESS PERSON.

So, you might be asking how you can maintain the balance. The answer is *grace*. Grace is there to help you when you mess up. The word *grace* appears over 125 times in the New Testament alone! That means that grace is an important topic to God, and He wants you to know about it.

The Greek word for *grace* means "the divine influence upon the heart, and its reflection in the life."[1] In other words, grace is

God's help. If you let Him, God will literally help you make the right choices. You still won't be perfect, but you'll look more like Jesus every day. And when you do mess up; if you fess up, God will forgive you and get you back on the right track.

GOD DOESN'T WANT YOU TO CONTINUE LIVING RECKLESSLY AND TAKING HUGE RISKS JUST BECAUSE HIS GRACE IS THERE TO HELP.

When you repent and do a 180° turn away from sin, God will help you head back in the right direction. And just like the definition of *grace* said earlier, it should reflect this change in your life. In other words, people will be able to *see* grace working in and through you! For example, maybe you often lost your temper before you became a Christian. With grace, God will help you learn how to remain calm no matter what you're facing. Your friends and family will notice how you don't lose your temper like you used to. That is the reflection in your life of how grace is working in your heart.

Since walking in God's grace is a "balancing act," let me

mention the other side of it. While God wants you to lean into His grace and not beat yourself up about your failings, He also doesn't want you to abuse His grace. How can someone abuse His grace? The Bible puts it this way: "Well then, should we keep on sinning so that God can show us more and more of his wonderful grace? Of course not! Since we have died to sin, how can we continue to live in it?"[3]

To put it another way, grace is not your get-out-of-jail-free card. If you have ever played Monopoly, you know what I mean. There are several cards you can draw in the famous board game, and one of the cards is the Get Out of Jail Free card. I don't know about you, but when I have that card in my possession, I play the game a little more recklessly. I'm not worried about taking huge risks with the roll of the dice because I know that if I land on a space or do anything that would put me in jail, I can just present the card to the banker and get right out.

God doesn't want you to continue living recklessly and taking huge risks just because His grace is there to help. Remember, repenting is doing a 180° turn; it's about thinking and acting differently than you did before you became a Christian. So don't *knowingly* and *willingly* go to that party where you know you'll be tempted to do some bad things just because you know you can ask for forgiveness about it later. Don't fool around with your boyfriend or girlfriend because you want to enjoy the pleasure that comes from it, while thinking that after you feel guilty, you can just ask for forgiveness for what you did.

God knows your heart. You can fake it with people, but you can never fake it with God. Walk in the balance and blessing of God's grace by tapping into it when you need to but not abusing it when you want to. If you want to grow in your new faith in Jesus, you'll have to repent from some things. Remember, you're not the boss of your life anymore; Jesus is. You need to live a life based on what the Bible says.

That means you'll need to repent from things like gossip, swearing, doing drugs, lying, cheating, and premarital sex. Repenting is not just being sorry. Repenting is more than just asking for forgiveness. Repenting is a *lifestyle change*. It means you might need to change your friends, like we talked about earlier. You might need to stop listening to certain music or watching certain shows. You might need to cut some things out.

How do you know what you should cut out? Great question! Look inside yourself. Listen to your heart. Now that you're a Christian, Jesus can speak to your heart and help you make the right decisions. The world calls it your conscience. The Bible calls it your spirit. Now that you're a Christian, your spirit is born again and can talk with Jesus. You have always known the difference between right and wrong, even somewhat before you became a Christian. Now you not only know the difference between right and wrong, with God's help, you know the *best* way to go.

The Bible will also help you learn what you should cut out of your life. Remember, the Bible is God's love letter to you. It's everything He wants you to know about life. The B. I. B. L. E. is His **B**asic **I**nstructions **B**efore **L**eaving **E**arth. The Bible will show you which lifestyle choices are right and wrong. It will show you what kind of thinking is good or bad. It will teach you what type of language is helpful or hurtful. The Bible will even show you what kind of friends to make.

THE CATERPILLAR AND THE BUTTERFLY

Another way to look at repenting is to think about the caterpillar and the butterfly once again. Remember our analogy of these two creatures from an earlier chapter? If you look hard enough in the summer, you might find a caterpillar in your backyard. Some people like caterpillars, and some people don't.

AN IMPORTANT STEP IN YOUR NEW FAITH IN JESUS IS TO TURN AWAY FROM YOUR OLD WAY OF LIVING.

Caterpillars come in all shapes and sizes. Some are fat and plump; others are thin and smaller than a coin. Some are furry, and others have spots. But one thing they all have in common is that they slowly crawl to their destination. All caterpillars must crawl on their little feet to get where they're going, and it takes a long time.

Butterflies, on the other hand, can move around much more quickly. Butterflies fly from one destination to another in a matter of seconds. They're also able to get a better perspective of things. While caterpillars crawling around on the ground can't see the dangers ahead of them, butterflies can soar up above whatever lies in front of them. They can see the danger and avoid it.

Be like the butterfly. Stop acting like caterpillars, or as the Bible says, "Don't copy the behavior and customs of this world, but let God transform you into a new person by changing the way you think. Then you will learn to know God's will for you, which is good and pleasing and perfect."[4]

Another version of this verse says, "Be transformed." The word *transformed* comes from the Greek word *metamorphoo*.[1] Do you remember that word from our earlier discussion? Do you remember what it means? *Metamorphosis* is defined by Webster's as "a typically marked and more or less abrupt developmental change in the form or structure of an animal (such as a butterfly or a frog) occurring subsequent to birth or hatching."[5] Another definition from Webster's is a "change of physical form, structure, or substance especially by supernatural means."[5] Most of us learned about metamorphosis when we were taught how a caterpillar turns into a butterfly.

I believe that God created this process in nature to show us how an ugly, slow caterpillar crawling around in the dirt can turn into a beautiful creature—a creature envied by people, collected by some, and considered beautiful by most; a creature which can soar high above the ground with the beautifully painted wings God gave it.

To repent is to do a 180° turn. To do a one-eighty is to turn completely away from something. An important step in your new faith in Jesus is to turn away from your old way of living. Turn away from your old way of thinking. Stop repeating the same old habits and sins you did before you became a Christian. In other words, stop acting like a caterpillar. God has turned you into a beautiful butterfly. It's time to start acting like one.

Now that you know how to do a 180° from your old ways and understand what repentance means, let's *dive in* to our next step. Let's talk about taking the plunge.

6

TAKE THE PLUNGE

Get water baptized.

So now, what are you waiting for? Get up, be baptized, and wash away your sins as you call upon his name.

Acts 22:16 TPT

One of the most important events you can take part in after you get saved is getting water baptized. While being water baptized has no control over whether you spend eternity in heaven, it is a marked moment in your life that you'll never forget. Plus, it's a public display to your friends and family of the decision you made and the change that took place inside you. Many people say that water baptism is an outward expression of an inward change.

Think of water baptism the same way you would a high-school-graduation ceremony. As a student, you'll go through roughly 12 years of school. Over those years you'll learn how to read and write, how to do math, and how to solve scientific problems. You'll learn American history and world history, and you might even learn another language. The skills you learn from your schooling are determined by which classes you complete. If you're successful and have completed all the requirements to graduate, you get your diploma. The high-school diploma is a piece of paper that confirms what you accomplished.

As a senior in high school approaching graduation day, you have the option to participate in your high-school-graduation ceremony. There is a lot that goes into the ceremony. You must order a cap and gown, send out invitations to your family, and get your senior pictures taken. The school also has a lot of planning to do. They must set up an auditorium with an elaborate stage, schedule a commencement speaker, select a valedictorian, and put together a ceremony or program.

It's said that graduation ceremonies are filled with pomp and circumstance—whatever that means! The point is that they're fancy and memorable. And if you've done everything you need to, you can be a part of it. You can probably picture it now (if you haven't already done it). Graduation night arrives, and everyone files into the auditorium. Your family is there with their smart phones in hand to capture the moment. The speeches are delivered, the music is played, and eventually you make your way across the stage as they announce your name over the public-address system. You shake hands with the principal as you grasp your diploma.

With all of this in mind, I have one question for you: would you have still graduated high school had you not attended the graduation ceremony? The answer is *yes*! The graduation ceremony is not what makes you a high-school graduate. The completion of your schooling is what makes you a high-school graduate. In other words, the graduation ceremony is an outward expression to your friends and family of what you have already accomplished. Water baptism is similar in that it is an event or ceremony for your friends and family to watch. The ceremony is an outward expression of what already happened to you on the inside of your heart.

THE CEREMONY IS AN OUTWARD EXPRESSION OF WHAT ALREADY HAPPENED TO YOU ON THE INSIDE OF YOUR HEART.

There are two reasons you're encouraged to get water baptized after you decide to be a Jesus follower. The first reason is so that you can celebrate with your family and friends, and the second is because the Bible encourages you to. First, you want to celebrate with your family and friends the decision you made for Jesus. There are lots of things you celebrate in life, like birthdays, graduations, winning the state championship, or attending prom or homecoming. Since you're proud of your accomplishment or excited about the event, you invite family and friends to celebrate with you.

Now think about this: deciding to live for Jesus is *the* greatest decision you can make in life. This one decision has an eternal impact. That means that it's something that lasts well beyond this life here on earth. All the other things I mentioned are temporary; they don't last forever. If you invite your family and friends to celebrate with you in all the temporary things, wouldn't it make sense to invite them to celebrate with you in this one big eternal thing? Since they probably weren't with you when you decided to make Jesus your Lord and Savior, they didn't get to celebrate with you at the time. But getting water baptized gives them the chance to celebrate with you.

Now think about this: deciding to live for Jesus is *the* greatest decision you can make in life. This one decision has an eternal impact. That means that it's something that lasts well beyond this life here on earth. All the other things I mentioned are temporary; they don't last forever. If you invite your family and friends to celebrate with you in all the temporary things, wouldn't it make sense to invite them to celebrate with you in this one big eternal thing? Since they probably weren't with you when you decided to make Jesus your Lord and Savior, they didn't get to celebrate with you at the time. But getting water baptized gives them the chance to celebrate with you.

The second reason to get water baptized is because the Bible encourages you to. Jesus, who is our example, got water baptized. All through the Bible, we see who Jesus is and what Jesus does. In a few ways, Jesus was our substitute; He took our place. But in a lot of ways, Jesus is our example. He shows us what we should do and how we should live.

BUT GETTING WATER BAPTIZED GIVES THEM THE CHANCE TO CELEBRATE WITH YOU.

If Jesus spent time praying, we should spend time praying. If Jesus gave, we should give. Since Jesus was water baptized, we should get water baptized! The Bible tells the story of His baptism in the book of Matthew:

Then Jesus went from Galilee to the Jordan River to be baptized by John. But John tried to talk him out of it. "I am the one who needs to be baptized by you," he said, "so why are you coming to me?"

But Jesus said, "It should be done, for we must carry out all that God requires." So John agreed to baptize him.

After his baptism, as Jesus came up out of the water, the heavens were opened and he saw the Spirit of God descending like a dove and settling on him. And a voice from heaven said, "This is my dearly loved Son, who brings me great joy."[1]

Not only does Jesus show us the example of getting water baptized, but the early church in the book of Acts does as well. We read several times where new Christians get water baptized: "Then Peter said, 'Surely no one can stand in the way of their being baptized with water. They have received the Holy Spirit just as we have.' So he ordered that they be baptized in the name of Jesus Christ. Then they asked Peter to stay with them for a few days."[2]

Part of the reason that the early church water baptized new Christians is because Jesus made it part of the Great Commission. If you haven't been in church very long, you might not be familiar with the Great Commission. The Great Commission is the order that Jesus gives His disciples right before He leaves earth to go up to heaven until His return. That commission doesn't stop *until* Jesus returns to earth. The church has taken responsibility for that commission ever since it was given.

Here is the commission: "Therefore go and make disciples of all nations, BAPTIZING them in the name of the Father and of the

Son and of the Holy Spirit, and teaching them to obey everything I have commanded you. And surely I am with you always, to the very end of the age"[3] (emphasis added).

I'll never forget early summer of 1999 when I graduated from high school. I was so proud of myself for surviving the gauntlet of selecting courses of study, passing exams, dealing with social drama, and all that homework! I knew a couple of people who gave up somewhere along the way and didn't graduate. Some of my classmates dropped out because they didn't want to put in the work. Others quit before graduation because of some major life event, like getting pregnant. But I made it! I planned on being handed a high-school diploma.

I wanted to share this moment with my friends and family. I wanted the people I knew and loved the most to celebrate with me by attending my graduation ceremony. My parents and grandparents were there. And, of course, all my friends were there because they were graduating too. It was one of the proudest moments of my life, and one I will never forget.

The event of getting water baptized can be just as

"TAKE the plunge!
you'll never REGRET it,
and you'll never
FORGET it."

memorable, if not more so. My pastor, Jeff Jones, tells every person getting water baptized that they will *never* forget the experience. He's right, I haven't forgotten my water-baptism experience. Once you find a church to attend, check with your pastor to see when they will do water baptisms. Most churches make a big deal out of water baptism and might even hold a special service for it. Many times, churches will water baptize multiple people, so check and see if you can get signed up as soon as you're ready.

Take the plunge! You'll never regret it, and you'll never forget it.

Let's look at your final step to take in your new faith; let's talk about draft day.

7

DRAFT DAY

Volunteer and give.

And the second is like it in importance: 'You must love your friend in the same way you love yourself.'
Matthew 22:39 TPT

Put your heart and soul into every activity you do, as though you are doing it for the Lord himself and not merely for others.
Colossians 3:23 TPT

One of my favorite sporting events to watch is the NFL draft. There's a movie called *Draft Day* that does a great job showing all the behind-the-scene things that take place within the management of an NFL team on draft day. Lots of negotiations are had, contracts are written, and large sums of money change hands. All of this is done while the team is "on the clock," as they have a limited amount of time to decide before the next team makes their pick. It looks like a stressful and intense process, the goal being to put together the best possible team to compete in the NFL in the following football season.

As the clock winds down, the team who is in the "hot seat" makes their final decision on who they want to draft during that round. The pick is decided and is handed to the NFL commissioner who announces it to everyone in attendance and everyone watching on TV. Once a name, or pick, is announced, that person gets to take the stage and is often presented with a jersey of the team that selected him. From that day on, the person who is drafted is part of the team.

There are some huge benefits to playing in the NFL. Some of the more well-known and talented players earn massive salaries

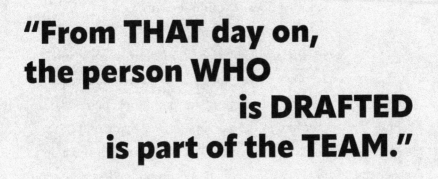

"From THAT day on,
the person WHO
                is DRAFTED
        is part of the TEAM."

ranging in the millions. If that player is elite in his skills compared to the rest of the football league, he could even score some sponsorships with big-name companies like Nike and Gatorade. A few months after the draft is completed, the season begins. Fans across the country get to watch as the talented pick sits on the sidelines reading a good book.

Wait. Something doesn't sound right about that.

Of course that isn't right! If an NFL team spends time scouting and recruiting a player, and then they invest millions of dollars to draft him, they aren't going to want him sitting on the sidelines. They want him in the game playing as many minutes as possible to help the team win games. He is expected to show up to every practice and every game suited up, conditioned, and in good health ready to go.

You may not be an elite athlete. You may not even be an average one. And I'm sure that if you're reading this book, it's not because you were just drafted into the NFL. If you were, let me know. I'd like to get your autograph! But, when you decided to make Jesus the Lord and Savior of your life, you were, in a sense, drafted into His team. That team is made up of "players" in churches all around the world. The "game" is eternity, and lives are at stake.

HE IS EXPECTED TO SHOW UP TO EVERY PRACTICE AND EVERY GAME SUITED UP, CONDITIONED, AND IN GOOD HEALTH READY TO GO.

You were probably given the chance to make Jesus the Lord of your life because of other people who were drafted to this worldwide team. Maybe it was a greeter at church that made you feel welcome. Maybe the worship music touched your heart, which couldn't have happened without the worship team. Maybe someone prayed with you at church. Or maybe it was the message the pastor shared with you. Whatever the case, someone was willing to show up and play hard so that you were given the opportunity to get "drafted" by Jesus.

LOVE, SERVE, GIVE

Now, it's your turn. The final step of this book is all about draft day. The plan is for you to take all the other steps and position yourself to *love*, *serve*, and *give*. As you attend church regularly, choose your friends wisely, repent from your old ways, and read your Bible and pray every day; you'll grow in your faith and begin looking a lot more like Jesus. Part of looking more like Jesus is by loving, serving, and giving.

Love Like Jesus - Even though you may have *just* become a Christian, I'm sure you're familiar with the Ten Commandments. Most people are familiar with them, even if they don't live by them. Back when Jesus was on the earth, He had many people ask Him many questions. There was one specific time when a group of Pharisees tried to trip up Jesus with a question. The Pharisees were religious people of Jesus' day, and they tried to live strictly by the law.

As you read through the Gospels, you'll see that often the Pharisees tried to trip up Jesus. They didn't like Him and the message He shared. They didn't believe Jesus was who He said He was, and so they thought everything Jesus taught was wrong. During this specific time, a Pharisee asked him, "Teacher, which commandment in the law is the greatest?"[1] The Pharisee was asking Jesus: of the Ten Commandments, which one was the most important to follow? He knew that there was no correct answer because whichever one Jesus chose would be wrong. That's because all of the commandments were seen as equally important or great.

Jesus' reply stunned the Pharisee. (Jesus always stunned the Pharisees!) He said, "'Love the Lord your God with every passion of your heart, with all the energy of your being, and with every thought that is within you.' This is the great and supreme commandment. And the second is like it in importance: 'You must love your friend in the same way you love yourself.'"[2]

In other words, Jesus said that love is the most important thing, the most important commandment. Jesus blew the Pharisees away! He didn't pick just one commandment like they thought He would; instead, He taught everyone to look at obedience in a different way. That is, He showed them that love covers everything. Jesus showed the Pharisees that if a person lives their life loving God and loving others, they will obey *all* the commandments by default.

If a person loves God, they won't use His name in vain. If a person loves other people, they won't steal or kill. Jesus had a lot to say about love. You can find it in John 14-17. Jesus knew that His time on earth was almost up. Naturally, a person shares their most important words with those they love when they know they're dying. Jesus knew He was about to go to the cross, so He made sure He focused on what was most important. He spoke about love repeatedly with His disciples. He said, "I love each of you with the same love that the Father loves me. You must continually let my love nourish your hearts. If you keep my commands, you'll live in my love, just as I have kept my Father's commands, for I continually live nourished and empowered by his love."[3] He not only packaged obedience to all the commandments within love, but He also talked about it with His disciples just before He left earth. He called it one of the most important things in life.

Later in the Bible, we see John writing about this same love Jesus talked about, "The beautiful message you've heard right from the start is that we should walk in self-sacrificing love toward one another."[4] He also wrote, "Yet we can be assured that we have been translated from spiritual death into spiritual life because we love the family of believers."[5] In other words, the mark of a true Christian is that he or she loves people. Now that you have made Jesus the Lord and Savior of your life, you should love *all* people, everywhere, always.

Loving people can be difficult. It is especially difficult when we must love our enemies or love people who have hurt us. But remember what I talked about in the chapter about repentance: God's grace will help you! Loving people means treating people kindly and fairly. It means treating people equally. Loving people means forgiving people just as Jesus forgave you. Loving others is one of the three things you need to do to play on this worldwide team known as the Church. Remember, lives are at stake. The Church needs all hands on deck, and we need you to play to win!

IN OTHER WORDS, THE MARK OF A TRUE CHRISTIAN IS THAT HE OR SHE LOVES PEOPLE.

Serve Others - You might be asking the question: *how* do I love others, or *what* does it look like to love others? Those are both good questions. I already said that loving people means treating them kindly, fairly, and equally. It also means forgiving people when they have done you wrong. We are to love people no matter what they look like, where they came from, or what they believe. If you can live by this standard, it will address *how* to love most people. In answering *what* that love looks like, we should again look to Jesus. He is our example.

DID YOU KNOW THAT YOUR CHURCH HAS A LOT OF WORK TO DO YET NOT A LOT OF HANDS TO HELP?

Jesus once said, "For even the Son of Man came not to be served but to serve others and to give his life as a ransom for many."[6] We can see Jesus serve people throughout the New Testament. He went about doing good for people, healing them, and helping those in need. One of the most beautiful examples of Jesus serving others was when He washed the feet of His disciples. In looking at the life of Jesus, we can see that a great place to *show* love is by serving others. "Dear children, let's not merely say that we love each other; let us show the truth by our actions."[7]

A great place to begin demonstrating your love for others is by serving them. And a great place to start serving others is in your church. Did you know that your church has a lot of work to do yet not a lot of hands to help? Jesus puts it this way, "The harvest is huge. But there are not enough harvesters to bring it in."[8] Churches are full of hurting people who need help. Churches exist within communities of people who need a lot of support. Most churches are overworked and understaffed. They need you.

As you take this final step of your newfound faith and respond to your draft day, consider how you might be able to help your church. Check with your church or youth group to see where they need volunteers. Most churches have several places you can volunteer, and they have a process you can go through to become approved to serve. From greeting people at the door to helping in the parking lot, from serving as an usher to teaching kids, there is plenty of work to do! As you grow in your faith by attending church and choosing your friends wisely, you'll be ready to serve. As you spend time reading your Bible and praying, you'll develop the skills needed to help.

Give - You've learned about loving and serving others, now let's wrap up with the process of giving. The Bible has much to say about giving, specifically tithing to your local church. There are different ways of giving: giving of your time, giving of your skills, and giving of your money. I'm not going to go into detail on the biblical idea of the tithe; it's not the purpose of this book. I'd encourage you to connect with your pastor on this topic to get further direction. For now, I just want to briefly mention what the tithe is and then encourage you to give as part of your newfound faith.

The idea is rather simple. Everything good comes from God. God owns *everything*. Since He is a good and loving Father, He blesses us as His children with good things. One way that He blesses us is through material goods and financial resources. In response, we honor God and demonstrate our love and appreciation to Him by giving back some of what He has given to us. Not only do we do this out of love and appreciation *to* Him, but we also do it out of faith and trust *in* Him. But you might wonder what you should give Him and how you get it to Him. Let's start by looking at how people used to do this in the Bible.

FIRSTFRUITS

Check out this scripture from Proverbs: "Glorify God with all your wealth, honoring him with your firstfruits, with every increase that comes to you."[9] Back in the day when Proverbs was written,

societies were very agrarian. *Agrarian* means that they were focused
on and relied heavily on farming. Look at that! You're learning big
words!

THE IDEA IS RATHER SIMPLE. EVERYTHING GOOD COMES FROM GOD. GOD OWNS EVERYTHING.

There was no such thing as the Industrial Revolution yet.
The technological and informational revolutions hadn't happened yet
either. People didn't work daily nine-to-five jobs in office buildings.
A person's wealth was largely determined by what they planted and
harvested or by what kinds of and amounts of animals they owned.
If you happened to own lots of cows back then, you were richer than
someone who owned no cows. If you planted a crop and ended up
with large quantities of it at harvest time, it was like earning a large
paycheck.

Now that you understand how wealth was measured back
then, Proverbs 3:9 makes more sense. The writer is saying that

whatever you earn, whether its cattle or crops, give God the first bit of it. And every time you receive an increase in your wealth, give Him the first of that too. In other words, if you gain four more cows, give a portion of the cows back to God. The Bible teaches us to give God the first of whatever we earn. The Bible also gives us more detail on how much of the "firstfruits" we should give.

Malachi 3:10 says, "'Bring all the tithes into the storehouse so there will be enough food in my Temple. If you do,' says the Lord of Heaven's Armies, 'I will open the windows of heaven for you. I will pour out a blessing so great you won't have enough room to take it in! Try it! Put me to the test!'" The *tithe* simply means 10 percent, so the Bible teaches that from whatever we earn, we should give the first 10 percent of it back to God. Again, God owns everything, even what we earn. He is the one who blesses us with what we earn. Our giving back the first 10 percent to Him is not because God will go broke without it; it's done to remind us of His goodness and His role as our source of everything.

So now you know that God owns everything, and that He blesses you with a portion. You also know that the Bible teaches that you're to give back to God the first 10 percent of whatever you earn.

But how do you give it back to Him? The previous verse you read tells us to bring it to the storehouse. As Christians, we believe that the storehouse is the local church. In other words, we are to give back to God the first 10 percent of what we earn by giving it to our local church. While God doesn't *need* your money, your local church does need financial resources to operate.

THE BIBLE TEACHES US TO GIVE GOD THE FIRST OF WHATEVER WE EARN.

Part of your role in loving, serving, and giving is to financially support the church you attend. Churches must pay the light and heating bills. They must pay the salaries of the staff that work at the church. When your youth group puts on a big event with games and food, it costs money. Every time the church holds a coat drive or donates bikes to kids in need, it requires financial resources. When you give 10 percent of what you earn to your church, you're not only honoring and trusting God but you're also investing in eternity through what your local church does with those funds.

I understand that not everyone has a job, and some young people don't earn an income. Remember, until you're in a position where you can financially support your church, you can still give of your time and your skills. That's why draft day is about loving, serving, *and* giving. The point is to take everything you're learning and receiving as a new Christian, and turn around and help others with it. You do this through your local church.

It's game time! Get out there, and help the team win!

AN INTRODUCTION TO FIRE UP

Before I conclude *Now What?* and challenge you to put its steps to work in your life, I wanted to share one final step I personally believe is vital in the life of every Jesus follower. The subject matter has been a controversial topic between denominations since the church began. It remains controversial today.

Because of this, I wanted to write a separate book for those of you who were interested in studying it further. For those of you who aren't, simply don't read the book. I appreciate the fact that students from all kinds of denominations will read *Now What?* and I don't want you to dismiss me as an author or dismiss the biblical content I present based on my views in this one area.

In my book *Fire Up*, I cover the topic of the baptism of the Holy Spirit. The book is written much like *Now What?* in that it tries to speak to the topic in a way that young people can understand, while communicating as many practical details as possible. Let me be clear; I am a firm believer in the baptism of the Holy Spirit as a follow-up event to a person making Jesus their personal Lord and Savior. I also believe that the evidence of this event is a person speaking in different tongues or languages.

There are great benefits to this experience, as well as, several misconceptions. In *Fire Up*, I lay all of them out on the table for the reader to study for themselves. No matter where you personally stand on this topic, I would encourage you to talk to your pastor about it and learn what your church believes. And I would encourage you to study the Bible for yourself and pray about this topic, just like I would expect you to with anything else.

I'll leave you with this bit of advice I learned from Bible school; it's helped guide my belief system in all Bible topics—be like the Bereans. The Bereans were a group of people that lived during the time of the Apostle Paul. Because they were around when Paul was teaching, they benefited from sitting under his instruction. The book of Acts says, "The people of Berea were more open-minded than those in Thessalonica, and they listened eagerly to Paul's message. They searched the Scriptures day after day to see if Paul and Silas were teaching the truth."[1] I encourage you to do the same with this topic and with the entire you book you're about to finish. *Now What?* lays out plenty of direction and encouragement, and it includes dozens of Bible verses. Study everything for yourself, pray about it, and let Jesus lead you.

CONCLUSION

But don't just listen to God's word. You must do what it says. Otherwise, you are
only fooling yourselves.
James 1:22 NLT

You've done it! You made it through this book. Now, take
your right hand, place it over your left shoulder, and pat yourself on
the back. Well done! I hope and pray that this book has helped you
make sense of the recent decision you made for Jesus. I trust it has

given you some practical steps on what you can do to keep your new faith growing and moving in the right direction. This book wasn't designed to be read once and then placed on a shelf. This book is here for you to pick back up whenever you feel like you need some help and direction.

DO WHAT YOU READ IN THE BIBLE, AND WATCH YOUR LIFE EXCEL IN WAYS YOU NEVER THOUGHT POSSIBLE.

I'll leave you with one last Bible verse. I had a pastor teach this verse to our Sunday school class when I was a Bible-school student. It's one of my favorite verses in the whole Bible, and I read it often. It comes from the book of James, "But don't just listen to God's word. You must do what it says. Otherwise, you are only fooling yourselves."[1] In the previous chapter, I encouraged you to be like the Bereans—study everything you learn from spiritual leaders. In addition to studying what you hear, I challenge you to put it into practice.

You're not supposed to read the Bible just to gain some head knowledge. While you will gain head knowledge from reading the Bible (just like when you read any other book), the Bible will bring you much more! It's an instruction manual on how to live this thing called life. Don't just read the Bible and forget what you read. *Do* what you read in the Bible, and watch your life excel in ways you never thought possible.

I'd encourage you to do the same with *Now What?* as a companion to your Bible. Don't just read about the steps; live them out. Start attending church. Choose your friends wisely. Read your Bible every day. Spend time in prayer and worship every day. Do a 180° turn from things you shouldn't do. Get water baptized, and start loving, serving, and giving! Saying *yes* to Jesus is the greatest thing you'll ever do in your life. Don't let your *yes* be just a moment in time; let it be for the rest of your life.

APPENDIX

POPULAR WORSHIP ARTISTS

As I mentioned in chapter four, I have provided you with a list of popular worship artists to help you create your own personal worship playlist. This list is by no means all inclusive. There are hundreds of worship artists to choose from that I don't have the time or room to include. I am not personally endorsing any of the ones on this list, but simply included them based on their popularity and availability at the time of the writing this book.

There are several genres of music styles within worship music. I did my best to include several of those styles. In time, you'll find what genre you connect with the best. The point here is to encourage you to get your playlist created and begin spending time in your own personal worship with The Lord.

- Brandon Lake
- Capital City Music
- Cody Carnes
- Elevation Worship
- Highlands Worship
- Hillsong
- Housefires
- Jesus Culture
- Jubilee Worship
- Kari Jobe
- Leeland
- Maverick City Music
- Passion
- People & Songs
- Red Rocks Worship
- SEU Worship

- The Belonging Co
- UPPEROOM
- Vertical Worship

END**NOTES**

Introduction
1. John 3:7
2. 1 Thessalonians 5:23
3. 1 Peter 3:4 NKJV
4. Proverbs 4:23

Chapter One
1. *Merriam-Webster.com Dictionary*, s.v. "worship," accessed January 10, 2022, https://www.merriam-webster.com/dictionary/worship.
2. Psalm 92:13 NKJV
3. Matthew 4:4

4. Psalm 34:19
5. Proverbs 3:6

Chapter Two

1. 2 Corinthians 5:17
2. Galatians 2:20
3. Proverbs 13:20
4. Matthew 7:16
5. Galatians 5:22-23
6. Proverbs 4:23
7. Matthew 28:19 TPT
8. Matthew 5:14-16 TPT

Chapter Three

1. *The World Factbook*, s.v. "Zambia," accessed January 10, 2022, https://www.cia.gov/the-world-factbook/countries/zambia/.
2. *The World Factbook*, s.v. "United States," accessed January 10, 2022, https://www.cia.gov/the-world-factbook/countries/united-states/.
3. Matthew 4:4 MSG
4. Barna Group, *Gen Z – The Culture, Beliefs and Motivations Shaping the Next Generation*, (Ventura: Barna Group, 2018), 13.
5. Barna Group, *Gen Z – The Culture, Beliefs and Motivations Shaping the Next Generation*, 40.
6. Barna Group, *Gen Z – The Culture, Beliefs and Motivations Shaping the Next Generation*, 53.
7. Joshua 1:8
8. 2 Timothy 3:16
9. Colossians 3:15 AMPC
10. Isaiah 40:22
11. Romans 12:2
12. Matthew 5:44 TPT
13. Psalm 119:105

14. Hebrews 4:12
15. 1 Peter 3:9
16. Proverbs 26:20
17. Galatians 5:22-23
18. Galatians 5:19-21

Chapter Four
1. Numbers 23:19
2. Isaiah 55:10-11
3. Luke 5:16 NIV
4. Philippians 4:6
5. John 14:14
6. James 4:2
7. Foster, Richard, *Celebration of Discipline,* (New York: Harper Collins, 1978), 158.
8. Matthew 4:10

Chapter Five
1. Strong, James, *Strong's Exhaustive Concordance of the Bible,* (Nashville: Thomas Nelson, 1990).
2. 2 Timothy 2:22
3. Romans 6:1-2
4. Romans 12:2
5. *Merriam-Webster.com Dictionary,* s.v. "metamorphosis," accessed January 3, 2022, https://www.meriam-webster.com/dictionary/metamorphosis.

Chapter Six
1. Matthew 3:13-17
2. Acts 10:46-48 NIV
3. Matthew 28:19-20 NIV

Chapter Seven

1. Matthew 22:36 TPT
2. Matthew 22:37-39 TPT
3. John 15:9-10 TPT
4. 1 John 3:11 TPT
5. 1 John 3:14 TPT
6. Matthew 20:28
7. 1 John 3:18
8. Luke 10:2 TPT
9. Proverbs 3:9 TPT

An Introduction to Fire Up
1. Acts 17:11

Conclusion
1. James 1:22

MCCARTY MINISTRIES

Website

- Visit **www.mccartyministries.com** where you can:

- Contact Matt and Mia personally — they'd love to hear from you

- Book Matt and Mia for speaking engagements

- Shop for books and apparel

- Watch and listen to videos and podcasts from Matt and Mia

- Read blogs from Matt and Mia

- Follow their travel schedule

- And more…

Social Media

 mccartyministry

 mccartyministry

ABOUT THE AUTHOR

 Matt and his wife Mia founded McCarty Ministries in 2011. Their mission is to reach over 100,000 youth for Jesus, and train youth pastors all over the world. In pursuit of that goal, they spend much of their time traveling the United States sharing the message of faith in a culturally relevant way. Their style of teaching is full of passion and energy as they share Bible truths through the lens of our current culture. Matt and Mia share this message through speaking engagements, as well as through social media, podcasts, blogs, and books.

Matt is the author of several books, including kid's books about American history, heroes, and values, as well as faith-based books for youth. Matt is a graduate of RHEMA Bible Training College and is licensed and ordained through RHEMA Ministerial Association International. Matt earned his B.S. in Business Administration from Cornerstone University, and his M.B.A. from Liberty University. Matt and Mia live in Michigan with their three children.

CPSIA information can be obtained
at www.ICGtesting.com
Printed in the USA
JSHW040238020422
24416JS00002B/6